Into
the
arms
of the
Carers

Timothy

Draycott

The preface.

I write this in loving memory of my long term partner and mother to my children Amanda aged 40 when she sadly passed away April 2016 from the dreaded cancer and to my mother Susan who passed away due to a tuna on the brain April 2019 , I love you both so much .

Alas I have been informed that I must change names of some of the people I mention in this memoir, apparently they can sue me for telling the truth.

You may find some spelling mistakes as I find spell checker long and tedious, bad verbs and pronunciation may also occur often so I really do not think I'm going to win any literary prizes with this book.

There is a lot in the past that one doesn't recall until one see's it in front of them   , if you see what I mean , so I think this would make for a very interesting read ?.

I have no writing knowledge whatsoever , I got an O level in English Lit and language if that's anything to go by , I have not studied writing a book , I have taken no advice on writing a book , but I did look up the word prologue but didn't like the sound of it so preface it is .

Sit back drink brandy , which I think I'm immune to thanks to working for (in later life) Anthony Worral Thompson ,catering for our lovely Queen eliz the 2nd , president Mitterrand the GLORIOUS Maggie Thatcher xxx rip , and that's just naming the virtually unknown celebs .

Hopefully I will win the bet with my Amanda and then I will have to spend another 15 years remembering my later celebrity filled life. (Which could also be quite damning, but I would have to seek legal advice as everyone who I could mention is highly probably still alive, (apart from Bob Monkhouse)

I have inserted many pages from transcripts from councils, care workers, police and social workers.

Every word typed here is from the county council files I hold about my life from the age of 1.

I fill in the gaps on what I remember and boy, (heed this whoever be alive) do I remember and remember very very well. (As told very emotionally indeed to a Midlands BBC reporter in 2015).

I have spoken to all councils involved about the legality of what I am about to write.

Shropshire county council quoted "Print what you like, they did not even want their legal team to look at it? (I did tell them it was damning).

I know you will say at the end of this book, WHY, Do you not press charges on the perpetrators and abusers.

Well it's my word against theirs , bad of me but I really do not want to see frail men be sentenced to a prison sentence that late in life and to drag myself through a lengthy court hearing .

And I'm going to send a copy to each of the abusers (I know where 2 are) so they can die knowing that adult people are out there who remember.

I will mention the physical & sexual abuse in care homes ,(highlighted by the bbc in 2014 at (amongst others - St Gilberts school , Worcs , Besford house , Shrewsbury , The Mount , Wellington , Telford) youth custody , detention centre and prison from 1979-87 through 4 care homes , my parents constant barrage of abuse to each other and being placed on anti depressants when I was 11 (that was a shocker , but i later found out it was an anti bed wetting drug in them days but now in 2017 its an anti-depressant).

The constant running away on adventures (absconding) around the country (aged 11-16).

Driving and ringing cars at the age of 12/13 when I was 4.5".

You're going to laugh , highly probably cry , you will feel angry and like me when writing this it may send you into a small depression and please do not read this book if you are easily offended

 It's all here or may I say, it all starts over on the next page after i have mentioned that proceeds of this memoir go to Barnado's Abused Childrens Dept , A charity who do not pay hundreds of thousands to the Chairman but support thousands of children and young people who have experienced sexual abuse , purchasing this memoir will make them safer .

Chapter 1   AGED 1.10 (1st October 1968).

(The "don't worry it doesn't go on for long chapter".)

"My Mrs and our house are unfit for our kids can you do something ", my father basically said to Mrs Clarke the social services, oh they certainly did that.

I was probably goo gooing and poo pooing green at the time but Our Local health visitor Mrs Clarke after visiting said conditions were appalling and she recommended that the children be placed in care until better accommodation was found but the offer was firstly refused by my father when they visited) he probably thought that social services would help out financially or give us a new washing machine or something).

As mentioned they certainly did, this started my rollercoaster ride through early life so Unbeknown to me (until a few prior to writing this) I was placed in care when I was a 1 year old chubby child. (1968).

On 1st October 1968 they placed 3 out of the 4 of us in Cruckton hall, a child welfare home just outside Shrewsbury, Shropshire.

A place I have researched in great detail and come up with.....not a lot really.

My sister ,(aged 2) , my mid brother (aged 5) and myself aged just over 1 .

My eldest brother stayed at home due to him being at school already.

I weighed in for Cruckton at an amazing 30Lb, I had a cold in the head and I contacted measles only 15 days prior to the 19/10/68.

Discharged to my mother for a little while on the 23/12/68 (that was nice of them)

I tried to Research Cructon, Shropshire reference – PA3, SYSTEM XPA3).

But alas a 89 year wait ~ so apply to freedom of information , that will take a year – no time in my life I can wait for that to appear , so I will crack on .

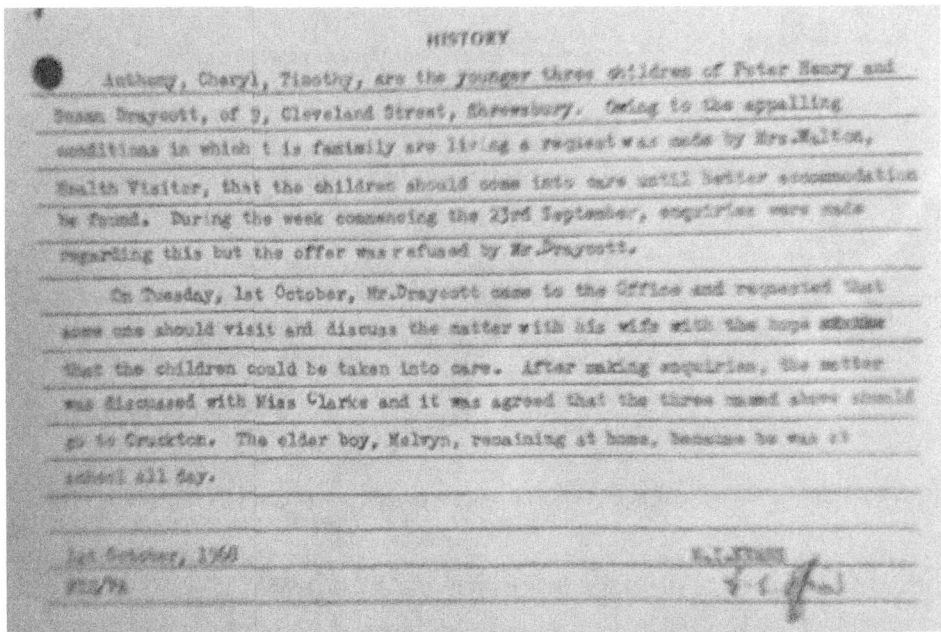

zsFather and mother had different places to live in 1968 due to the constant arguing and dads drinking, but this changed 6 months later when mother moved into one of my grandmother's houses. (Gran had 3 houses at that time, one of them being the plush Abbey lodge B&B on Abbey Foregate, stone columns either side of the main door, massive bay windows and always full of flowers on one of the busiest roads into Shrewsbury.

My gran was renowned for her flowers in the front (geraniums) she won the Shrewsbury flower show many times , meaning this gave us access to the flower show every year for free for years , just brilliant at the time .

(Later in life I used to raid my grans cellar for the vintage whiskey in this house and drink with my buddies on the roof, throw the empty bottles on top of the buses that passed on the main Rd, - Yes I was a naughty boy).

But what a lovely home it was my Nan got for my mother in Cleveland street , Shrewsbury (I visited it only last month , they have done well doing it up over 40 years).

My gran who was a good ole chunky women when past her 70's , with a bouffant hair style , usually pink or light purple or on some occasions lileekia blue , (*that's a mixed between lilac, leek & sky blue, smart dresses to wear , all pink , purple , green 70s style and oh so garish*).

Oh and the jag , oh wow twin tanks 4.2 light sky blue , leather seats throughout , plush as fuck and with ashtrays for every seat I'm sure .

 She made her money in bed and breakfast, she really wanted her daughter and my father to stay separated, I remember my gran telling me so many times when I used to go buy her ciggies when I was 12-ish "buy me 2 fags and Stay away from that father of yours, he's trouble ", (*Yeah Nan, I was 12, I really listened*).

But I can only really remember them words from Nan, all the trips to Barmouth, prestatyn and Ryle with her and Wilf and our family I do not remember conversations with my gran?

The shop we mainly went being Dot Allan's in Monkmoor road (now a hairdressers),

TimTim the Chinese takeaway now stands next door which used to be pui Hong Chinese takeaway, (pui Hong did the best chips, sometimes round in the shape of a football, and covered in sea salt which has since got very popular, I currently have around 6 different 1kg bags of edible coloured sea salts from around the world, mmm maybe a hidden fetish).

 Dot Allen had a twin sister and they lived in the small area in the back of the shop , them being around 60yrs old at the time , you never knew who was serving you (I'm sure they shared the same clothes) , they sold ciggies at 2p each and I'm sure all my family would agree that , as they also went shopping for mum and Nan at Dot Allan's shop , lovely fantastic women they were , but in a strange way , like witches looking down on you " oh yes my dear what is it you need today for nanny – 2 fags ?).

Ooh so creepy at the time but brings a smile to my face now?

Nans B&B was mainly for dossers who could only just afford to pay the £1 per night, no breakfast, my Nan loved cash and I remember her having a lot of it in the back of the kitchen cupboard and in the telephone draw in the big bay window, not once did I steal cash from my gran, I don't know why I just didn't?.

I'm going off track so back to Cruckton hall when I was nearly 2 years old.

My parents were being ordered to pay 36/3 rising to 4.9/0 - ? To the welfare of us children in Cruckton hall. (Visiting allowed by mother, supervised with father)

It was a voluntary and remand home from Jan 1964- DEC 31ST 1970.

Gather - National achieve (Kew) BN62/265

Closed /retained document

Former Ref CHR/1994/5/1

Salop (Shropshire) county council, Cruckton hall

Files Closed for 81 years due to it containing sensitive information that may cause distress or endanger a living person or his or her descendants.

I do have the files from Cruckton but they are hard to scan and mainly empty of knowledgeable content, I can type in faster what they say than try to copy and show you.

My mother and fathers relationship was truly a volatile relationship, which as a family now we thought our mother got a kick out of going out with ruffians. (I knew of 3)

Reading from my social reports from sept 1969 from Cruckton , 1 year after being admitted to Cruckton my father was sentenced to 6 months borstal for an unprovoked attack and punching our local vicar , causing an eye injury .*(Ref national newspaper archives – Shrewsbury – Peter Draycott)*

After being found guilty he ran away from the dock in the court house, hit a police man by slamming the door in his face. (I did similar to a lad in Wellingborough detention centre when I was 16 in Northants 20 years later , slamming a door in his face and throwing him in a laundry basket when he provoked me ,days were added to my sentence, if I remember I will tell you about that later , or just remind me if I don't).

Like me (Currently) at 6.5", my father was also a big chap and was feared in this town in the 60s /70s due to his unprovoked attacks and violence on pub goers.

My sister went back home to my mother's new house? In sultan Rd, Shrewsbury, mid 1969 and brother then went back home 1 year later. My whereabouts are unknown through paperwork if I find some in the 2000 page dossier I have from Shropshire council I will fill in the blanks later but this has taken me quite a few years to sort out since the BBC muggled it all up when they took it away for study.

Why I gave them all my files I really do not know but I'm sure they will keep them locked away until the investigation into St Gilberts boys home (chapter 22-ish) springs its ugly head up again , when they investigated it in around 2015 (it's just a matter of time really).

Hopefully the national archive will spring up some things regarding Cruckton when I made the request before corona virus set in March 2020, but I very much doubt it?

$\underline{\hspace{3cm}}$ *M. J. Ford*

Child Care Officer

On receipt of the letter from Mrs Draycott, dated the 3rd September, 1969, I contacted Mr Turner of G.R. & C.H. Wace, College Hill, Shrewsbury. Mr Turner confirmed that Mrs Draycott was the tenant of 1 Sultan Road and that in view of the Separation Order, which included a non-cohabitation clause, granted on the 25.8.69., she could legally turn her husband out of the house. He told me that he has already advised Mrs Draycott that she should remain in her house and should eject her husband, seeking the assistance of the police if necessary.

4th September, 1969

This morning I called to see Mrs Draycott. I found her to be at home with two of her neighbours. When the neighbours had departed into the kitchen, I explained that for the following reasons I were not prepared to accept any of her children into care. I explained that she and not her husband was the householder and in view of the non-cohabitation clause, she could legally eject him from the house. Mrs Draycott said that she was afraid of her husband and of what he would do to her should she try to put him out. I told her that if this was the case, she should enlist the aid of the police and that she should, when she approached them, take her rent book and Separation Order with her. I went on to explain that the solution was in her hands. Mrs Draycott said that she was in arrears with her rent and she did not intend paying it until such times as her husband had left. I said that she should pay the rent up to date as soon as possible as the only person that she was harming was herself.

Mrs Draycott, together with her neighbours, decided that she would approach the police and her solicitor to-day in order that Mr Draycott could be put out this evening. It was her intention to leave the keys with the police and then go with her children to her mother until after the eviction had been carried out.

5th September 1969.

Child care officer advises mother to remain in the house and to eject my father from sultan Rd, (he must of served his sentence), and go to the police about my father's abusive behaviour towards my mother and (remaining??) Children.

That following evening mother stayed in the care of her neighbours whilst the police ejected my father from the house, (non co-habiting clause and separation order) mother gave the police a set of keys as she believed father would come back and stay in the house.

Right , here we go , after all that tireless writing we can now get to my story ,I'm sure I do not have far to go as I know I can write at least 30 words an hour , I'm sure I can write this in a week .

Deep breath and sip of Shropshire's finest ale of Darwin's Origin from Salopian breweries.

Sip turned into gulping half the pint.

It all started for me in April 1974 (I was 7 yrs old)

When friends and family say to me How can you possibly remember when you were 7 , well I do as I have all the evidence in front of me , as mentioned I fill in the gaps on what the reports say , Obviously I do not remember everything as from 12 yrs old I was plied with the later mentioned drugs so brain frazzle occurred at times but I stick to what I know , I do not speculate on what may have happened or what I may have thought what happened , these are my memoirs that meaning these are my memories , this will also be sent to everyone mentioned in this book well before publication just in case I did get a fact wrong .

My mother was told in April 1974 by social services that they think I should be in another care situation being Stirchley School and to be assessed.

This due to me moving into my grand fathers house, Harold (My father's side) with my newly new found love of my parents (I believe they married again and will be mentioned later in the book) grandfathers house being in new park Close , Castlefields , Shrewsbury .

A cul-de-sac of 1950s house, everyone knew everyone, but I will mention that street a few times later on.

I was being very troublesome at the new school (Lancastarian, Beachalls lane, Castlefields, Shrewsbury).

Whilst to and fromming from mothers and grandmothers I ended up getting badly burnt in a house fire when I was 6 , a house in St Michael's Street , Shrewsbury .

I do not remember any of this at all , but I know it happened as I have a 18"x8" scar running down my left leg , my brother tony ended up with at least 75% Burns , very badly burnt , I do believe he died for a few minutes , luckily I got away with a large burn down my left leg , apparently this all related to mum moving into this house (you will read about a lot of moves of mothers , I'm lose track of all the moves , I'm thinking of writing a book on just my mother's past houses), an ember jumped from the open fire onto a mattress in the living room , but as mentioned I do not remember anything of the fire at all , so I have to bypass that part of my life . (Sheryl burnt her ankle, Mel burnt his wrist, tony died arose then I think died again later in life and brought back again, I'm sure he will tell me when he reads this , Ha - Tony Jesus Draycott).

I may not remember that but I do remember a year later distinctly stealing potato puffs from the tuck shop at the Lancastarian school and selling them for half the price in the playground aged 7-ish.

Kids queued up for me just before the tuc shop opened

While all where in class and I went to the toilet it seemed at the time a good chance.

Virtually every day I broke in to the tuc shop by pushing the top half of the barn style door as that what I seen Mrs brown do when we queued up for tuc, I raided the place and I raided it good, at 7 years old and all this wonderful factory of choclyness iv crammed my face and stuffed my pockets.

Mr Harper being our (best ever in the world) head master, he was the wisest man and I looked up (and still do) to him and think of him often, If only I would have listened to him more.

I think if I did thought I would be now in some mundane job in Shrewsbury instead of the employment I ended up with serving the Queen and high end celebs after I was 22.

Going back slightly, (only slightly) The Lancastarian school was a early 1800s building that originally stood where our main railway station is now, then in the late 1800s they moved it down the road, adjacent to the old canal basin, what a lovely dominating building it was, and still is, I learnt that in the lancs and I think that is all I learnt, oh apart from Mrs brown amazing body, now the school has been sold to developers to make 18 luxury apartments by 2021.

I have enclosed an Arial photo I purchased from the national archive so not have to pay rights for it, (well I hope not) photo of the children playing ring a ring of roses in the playground of the Lancs, Castlefields, slightly before my time at 1964.

You can see more on my face book page, it may not be around now but face book was a web page that all people, persons and others, oh and communities interacted on, amazing place on the web, but as I see into the future, it all got shut down now and is mainly an advertising platform and a place for people to upload what they had for tea or kids going to the first day of school.

Yeah Lovely.. Personally I preferred Don't stay in.com or MySpace , these new places have so many tracking cookies that even now as am uploading to a cloud ? Google will probably own the intellectual rights to what I have uploaded, I really do not know? (Do you?)

Buts it's scary.

Going off track does not do well for the memoir so I will, I promise, stay on track.

(The Lancs school bottom left) kids in the playground

The picture depicts the neighbourhood I was mainly in at the age of 7-9, look at that gorgeous dirty deep slate grey river (I swam in that a lot), I did have jabs later in life- honest

My report states a visit from my mother to the school to discuss this thieving problem I had.

Thieving problem, no way, a friend of mine 4 years my senior (I'm sure I will mention him plenty in future pages) says I used to pop to his house straight after school and wee on the 3 bar electric fire and go into hysterics when it crackled, then go to his mother's kitchen cupboard and steal food to take home (24/06/1974), On one occasion I stole a whole saxa salt 500g box and she plagued me for years to return it.

(I did eventually but as a piss take when I was over 21, wrote my name on the box and left it in the cupboard).

That house is 6th down on the terraced houses in the photo above xx

I was referred for mental health assessment or Social re-education. when I was 7 due to the troubles I was causing at school, I'm sure Mr Harper will remind me of what I got up to and I will end up writing another 30 pages so I best not send a copy to him but I was mainly encouraging others my age to do bad things (I'm sure they have that wrong, my mum said I was easily led)

Sundown county infants – 1 year

Timothy 7 years old is a well built lad dark hair and eyes , on tests he was seen to below average general intelligence , he has made a start on reading and writing which will need massively improving , Timothy tells me about his brothers (aged 13 , 9)and sister nearly 8 but says he has no daddy , he ran away .

Frequent stealing and lying occurs often in school, bullying and fighting with other children.

I understand the police have spoken to timothy regarding breaking into cars for food with another pupil, the family is known to the police and also social services.

Mother is antagonistic towards the school, in the circumstances I feel there is nothing more we can do, I have explained to him stealing is wrong (Yeah that worked)

There would appear to be a great deal of physical cruelty at home as Mrs Draycott admits to using the cane on Timothy when he is naughty and the boy is well cared for physically .

He frequently wets himself in school, he cries often when no cause to. (Ha, I still do)

If social services are involved with this family I suggest this report may be useful in the files of timothy (nice of you to say that Mr Walters and I'm glad you did as without it I would not be writing this) *, apologies about the scan below – they get better in age .*

25/04/74 - Social report - *On the referral from child guidance I have visited Mrs Draycott today to voice my concerns of the welfare of timothy as I have been informed that he rode a bicycle the opposite way down the town walls Road, one way street, after being approached by the constable his behaviour problems came into existence once again.*

I believe the psychiatric problems still exist.

(Massive apologies about the next scans , just wanted to show you how difficult they are sometimes) .

Intelligence   Attainment   Differential Diag.
WISC   WISC/WPPSI   BURT READING: 7.4 years   (see attached profile)

CA   7 - 8   VERBAL   SCHONELL SPELLING   TEST -

MA   6 - 4   PERFORMANCE   DANIELS & DIACK

IQ   89   FULL SCALE   READING -

                                                  SPELLING -

PSYCHOLOGIST'S OBSERVATIONS   Previous Psychological Report dated: N.I.

Timmy is a well-built lad with dark hair and eyes. Co-operation on the Binet
Test was adequate and he was shown to be of low average general intelligence.
He has made a start with reading and writing skills although he is not quite up
to average in this respect. In the family there are two older brothers,
Melvyn, aged 13, and Tony, aged 9, and one older sister, Cheryl, who is almost
8. Timmy also lives at home but Timmy told us that he hasn't got a dad - he left.

Frequent stealing and lying occurs in school, as well as some bullying and frequent
fighting with other children. Recently I understand he has been involved with
another lad taking food from cars which they broke into, and I understand the
police (and possibly the Social Services Department) may know the family on account
of this.

mother is antagonistic towards the school and would not accept child guidance.

In the circumstances there is nothing further that we can do although I have tried
to get across to Timmy the idea that stealing is quite wrong. There would not
be no great physical cruelty at home (although has been sent the stick at
when he is naughty) and the boy is well cared for physically. He does not
wet himself in the school situation but there has been no co-operation from
over this matter.

If the Social Services Department are involved with this family then
report might be a useful addition to their files. Nothing further
from the child guidance viewpoint.

I set fire to Sankeys home care centre (A DIY Warehouse being built in underdale Rd when I was 8 , not proud at all , no way , but I did phone 999 from the local phone box as I got paranoid about what granddad would say nearly blowing up a jcb , it was cold that night so me and a friend decided to light a fire under the jcb to keep warm, not thinking about the residents in all the houses adjoining in Tankerville Street(the police said that's how they got me , they said as the telephonist apparently recognized my voice (I think it was all local telephonist then) , and I think that's why in later life they did not pick me for the Hatton garden heist , Dumb and stupid juvenile I was).

MY GOD ...GIVE ME SHOCK THEREAPY WHY DONT YOU. I was 7-8 yrs old)

I realise through my Criminal record that I was charged with an offence of stealing a cycle in 1979 when I was 12 but I do not recall a bicycle in 74 ,but looking back on the lanc's reports(Lancastarian school)I did some naughty things .

One of my regrets I life was breaking into Malcolm's , Mr Chips chip shop in St Michael's street when I was around 10 yrs old and stealing a 30kg bag of spuds to take home while my mate was going for the 2 boxes of frozen sausages . (He always made his chips proper)

The police stopped us in their new rover 3.5, (later I would know it so well as I think in later life stole around 4-5 of them, 1 went over the top of Haughmond quarry).

So back to the (Ditherington Rd) chippie heist, the police stopped us, 2 juveniles walking up Ditherington Rd, Shrewsbury at 10.30 at night , (that 22.30 if your reading this and from the police force)

Hello, Hello, Hello they probably didn't say but I remember Brian saying that we have just come back from his grans as his dad shouted at him for not bringing home the spuds, so me and Brian went to get them from new park close (Eh – but that's my granddads house not his grans house) as we were so close to it and we had to walk all the way to Monkmoor he said (2miles away).

Wow, they only gave us a lift and dropped us straight outside Brians dads (police station being 500yrds away from brains house).

I lost my booty of a bag of spuds; I could not walk back to my granddads 2 miles away with that bag again.

The following day after school I went to Brians , his neighbour said his dad had taken him to a meeting (since researched) on freeing the picketers in Oswestry , 40 years later I get to know that it was Ricky Tomlinson the TV actor who was banged up and brians dad was involved in all that ruckus .

We got arrested (if you call it that) the following day when the report came in that a chip shop had been burgled, police had to do some thinking and earn their money as to who it was on that one.

As I remember Granddad in new park close not too pleased with me, his 2 giant red setters seemed to be displeased also, (rubbed off from granddad) and then the aviaries full of birds did not chirp at me, life was not good at this age as the bee's he had at his house didn't like me either, the fuckers stung me countless times.

We got a good telling off for the spuds and 20% meat sausage, what else could they do, I was 7

20/04/1975 – Social report

Visited and spoke to Mrs Draycott , the home seems to be very clean and Mrs. Draycott seems in a happy frame of mind now peter is comfortable with the children ,(He's obviously back – but not for long *) he has taken a real active interest in timothy's welfare .* (Yeah like I said not for long*)*

They now have a garden and all children seem in good moods as the house has finches and bullfinches in aviaries to keep the children occupied.

Mrs Draycott has a part time job which brings in a little additional money.

Also collected a gas cylinder loaned by the Dept some time ago?

(*Recently* found that the social services dept loaned mother a portable gas cooker as the gas supply was disconnected due to not paying the bill, slowly paying off the Arrears from a previous address also, report states only has a poor electric cooker at present, with only one ring working).

Family known to social services as we came to see timothy's brother's welfare.

17/03/1976 – Social report

Visited Timothy before school , very happy but seemed very off colour to go to school , I walked up with them , his mother has now started taking him to school due to him disappearing when he went alone or with his sister .

Mrs Draycott says she is thinking about marrying peter again as they all live next door to granddad (father's side).

Mrs Draycott says they all want to forget the past and move on.

Case discussed with Mrs Bailey – No further involvement seems to be warranted and none is required – Therefore CASE CLOSED.

Well that was a relief when I just read that, seems like my life is on the up.

The constant running away around this time was a lot of fun for me, swimming in the river with friends and on the infamous weir at midnight and beyond this time.

The newly built salmon run on the weir was a challenge, going up and down a thin width Shute made for fish to swim up , thick concrete.

The salmon Shute was obviously next to the river, rapid speed water and doing it at midnight made it all the fun.

I have since found out that approx 120-170, 000 litres of water go over the weir per minute.

We collected from the rubbish (not stole) massive cardboard boxes from the back of Dixons paint shop virtually next door to the Lancs and slept in them next to the river , as mentioned we stole the veg from the gardens surrounding the weir and cooked late at night , we even had corn on the cob cooked slowly over a fire made 20 yards from the weir , hidden in the trees , we did this many times though but I always tend to think of the sweet corn garden , I really should return a load of fresh veg to that gardens house as I feel and have felt quite guilty about it , they tended that garden very well and the sweet corn patch was only around 12 stems , so only 6ft x 6ft , that's not a lot of corn and we had it all .

On one occasion, myself, Karl and Steve were swimming at the top of the weir when the Bobbies (police) arrived, it was so dark and the torches they had not as powerful as nowadays could not really see us, so we started to make authentic quaking sounds. Qwaaark qwaaaark.

So authentic, I can still do the professionally sounding duck now.

The torches went over our heads as in the water and in the darkness our heads were just round objects in the river , wow that was a lucky escape , until Steve decided to do Unauthentic sounds QUACK , more of a piss take quack quack , well that was it we were collared but they had no way of getting us , we just swam to the other side , when they started to walk towards the bridge 300yrds up the river path, we started to walk across the top of the weir towards them , catch 22 fella's.

They gave up mostly in them days but now it's considered highly dangerous as Shrewsbury has lost loads of lives to the river in the Castlefields area, 2 I knew personally, 2 nearly lost.

Kids still swim in the weir but the salmon shoot is a no-go area, way too dangerous now.

On one occasion the Castlefields railway bridge was having its centennial painting job done on it, they parked a raft in the river in the centre of the bridge so no one could get to it.

Oh how wrong they were , we used to climb up to the large girders and circumnavigate the sticky out bits of buttress looking down on the river by holding onto large rivets , it was scary at times as you are 40-50ft above the river and virtually hanging on with 2 fingers , Fun when the river was in flood , the railway bridge has large round steel legs of around 20ft diameter going down into the river , we tied a rope we stole from the rail yard above our heads and climbed down to the raft which had a hut in the middle of the raft , this contained paint pots , a little gas stove and other shit a 12 year old would not be interested in .

It was a bit of time before we broke free of the chain attached to the bridge but we were free, we started to drift towards home and also the weir, the 30ft sloping waterfall 500 yards away.

We promised ourselves it would be fun until we got to the top of the weir, it started going over the top and we dived into the river at the top of the weir, thankfully we did as the raft started to break up, the shed fell off and toppled into the river and the raft took a nose dive, popped up and carried on down the river, oh well another adventure over, back to stealing bikes I think.

I did get caught scrumping from the vicarage next to the weir in Castlefields, Shrewsbury.

I vaulted the wall from the vicarage garden on to the river tow path so much that I caught my hand on the barb wire on top of the wall , the barb caught me on my wrist vein , my word , did it bleed , I nearly fainted .

If it was not for me getting back home so quick I'm sure I would have died but mum stuck a plaster on it and all was ok , I still have the scar reminding me to never steal from a vicar .

The gas works (which is now a housing estate) used to house large gas tanks which were an eyesore when the tanks where full of oil , 80-100ft high round tanks dominated the eye line in Castlefields , we played in here very often making dens , lighting fires against the oil tanks , and generally stealing from the vans .

On one night we did a triple heist, we robbed some vans in the British gas works depot in St Michaels street and stole crap, then went with the tools we stolen from them vans to the local newspaper warehouse outlet, Dawson news.

We popped the lock on the side door of the warehouse at the newspaper outlet (which ironically in another 30 years would be my own warehouse in my catering company, what a weird world I live I?)

We were confronted with thousands of comics in the newspaper outlet , with free toys on the front of the comics , this is heaven for a immature 11 year old , we grabbed as much as we could , this was better than the gas works , free Frisbees ,Dennis the menace plastic hand gloves where good for swaps at school , now I had the whole set , I remember having a pocket full of water squirters you place on your finger and hide it in your palm , I'm sure they were frogs ,plus we got a load of cheap girlie toys for the sister ., and again ironically I worked for Dawson News later in life and took the toys off the returning comics from newsagents and gave them to either charity or Parties I organised .

Then there was the BT depot in Ditherington, Shrewsbury.

Ditherington so named because the public used to Dither when watching criminals getting hung by the neck back in the day , I read of one really really bad criminal being hung for stealing a handkerchief , wow I would have been hung 1372 times in my 9 year crime spree.

But Oh what fun times we had at that age robbing the vans from British telecom (BT), stealing phones we knew nothing about as you had to attach them to the switch thingamajig underground, we just pretended we had mobile phones which we put to our ears at school pretending to phone home on the newest gadget, that's a quite a few years before mobile phones where invented, but I think Bodie and Doyle had something like that also.

Just down the road from BT was the Flaxmill , the world's first skyscraper , (which is now a museum to walk around so please visit if you can) , we played many times when 10-13 years old , it was mainly full of barley or wheat for the maltsters to brew beer , I thought

London was bad in my catering days working in old rail tunnels but the rats in the Flaxmill where humungous , I mean midget hippo size .

We used to chase them around the falloverable mountains of barley and on a couple of occasions I think (could have been more , could have been less) a friend brought his dads 22 air rifle and we would sit on the top iron girders (climb up the barley , 2nd floor up)in the maltsters (Flaxmill)and shoot the little bastards (would not dream of doing that now , I don't even swat flies to death or tread on bugs , I decided so late in life that life is life – regardless .

Chapter 2   My first years at school 04/09/1978 aged 11.6

(The learning to drink expensive whiskey chapter)

Belvidere Boys school, Shrewsbury

Immature , devious , unassuming and obtrusive , Ability and work standard well below average , close association with Andrew B , who he gets into trouble when they are alone but under supervision they cause no problems .(Alas my friend Andy passed away in 2017, as I'm sure he could have filled in many more gaps)

Constant thieving, his mother has been informed.

He cannot distinguish between sensible behaviour and conduct which inevitably is going to bring him into question , he exudes a pleasant innocent personality and does not seem too much concerned when he gets into fights , His grandmother who seems to look after Timothy tries to make excuses for him sayings " he's just a naughty boy but will grow out of it "it is very difficult to make Mrs Draycott come to terms with Timothy's problems she is very difficult to pin down on one point , she now finds it difficult in being firm with timothy ,she is aware of his associations and is trying to restrict it .

I feel she is overwhelmed by her son or she does simply prepared to turn a blind eye.

We had moved into a new house in Abbots green, Monkmoor I think due to the temptations living next door to my father's father, mum had met another man Richie.

The new house was only up the road from my new school

Richie was violent , he just came out of prison after meeting my father in prison , luckily I did not see him a lot as this is when social services decided to place me in care , but I do remember the fighting , shouting and us being placed at grandmothers quite a few times .

I thought I was on my best behaviour in these times but apparently not.

My first year at school were quite good apart from the box of Bullets I stole from a car in the safeways super markets car park , sold a few at school in singles , Thinking back on it now , very naughty . (Wow after looking for the last week I have found the report.

3RD April 1979, Inspector Jenkins – police liaison officers

(*"The above named boys went to the car park of safeways and took 200 rounds of ammunition from a car and also went back a second time to look for the Gun , the boys distributed the stolen ammunition to pupils at school which is how the incident came to the attention of the police.*

Mr Britnall (Andy who has recently passed away) stated that timothy wanted to go "Do some stuff" so Mr Britnall followed but did not steal the bullets from that car.

Mrs Draycott refused to let Timothy make a statement but both agreed that he took the ammunition & felt tip pen from the car but also admitted to taking a packets of crisps worth 30p from safeway (wow , I'm going up in the world , expensive crisps for the year ?).

Draycott has been involved in underage stealing and in review of this we feel Timothy should be prosecuted.

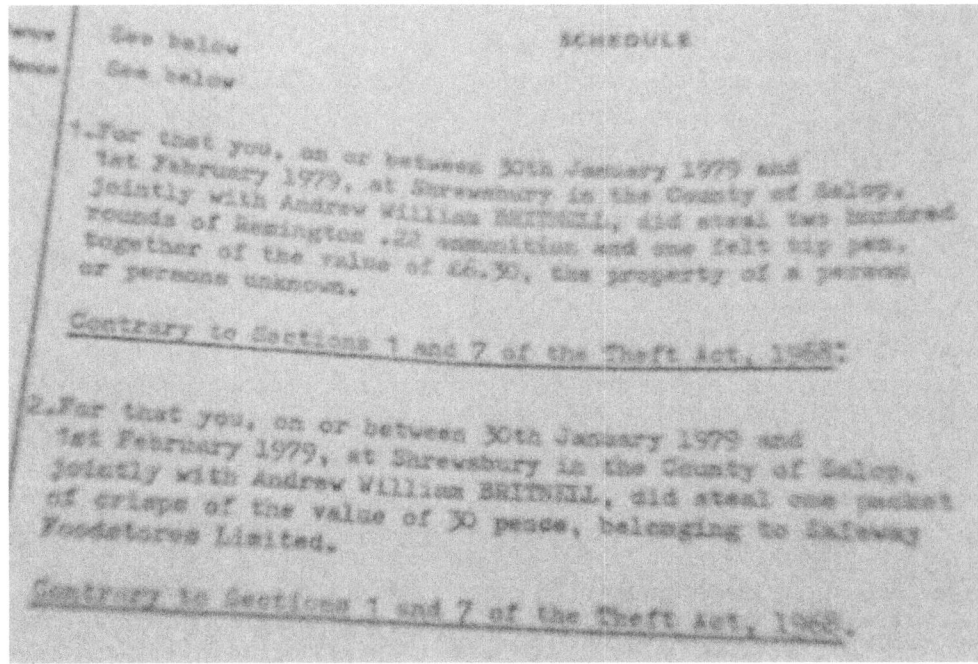

I was a little business man at school , my grandmother had a large conker tree in her bed and breakfast back garden so I gathered up the conkers and sold them in bags of 10 for 2p (enough for tuc for the day – spangles and crap like that).

I did cheat a bit and put needle holes in the shell to make them weaker so I would win a majority of the time, making me more money.

I was caned and given the slipper constantly for my behaviour, constant stealing from the local shop, stealing bikes was a big thing of mine at the time and selling them to the house gypsies who lived down the lane, they stripped them very quick as the school was around 200 yards away.

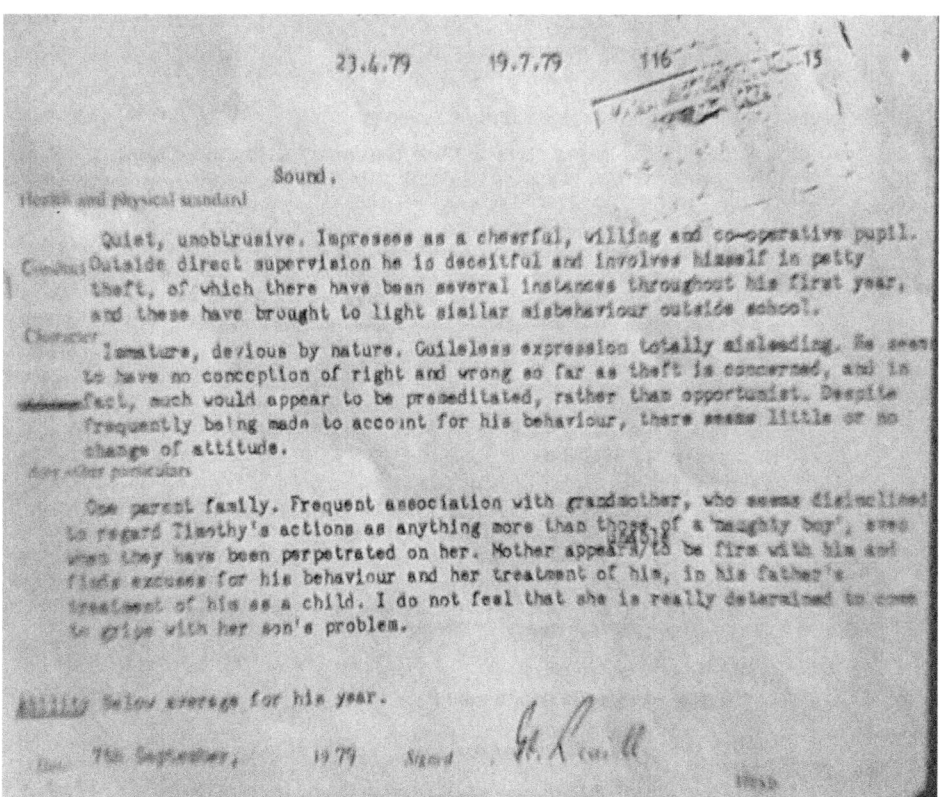

Sound.

Health and physical standard

Quiet, unobtrusive. Impresses as a cheerful, willing and co-operative pupil. Conduct Outside direct supervision he is deceitful and involves himself in petty theft, of which there have been several instances throughout his first year, and these have brought to light similar misbehaviour outside school.

Character

Immature, devious by nature. Guileless expression totally misleading. He seems to have no conception of right and wrong so far as theft is concerned, and in fact, much would appear to be premeditated, rather than opportunist. Despite frequently being made to account for his behaviour, there seems little or no change of attitude.

Any other particulars

One parent family. Frequent association with grandmother, who seems disinclined to regard Timothy's actions as anything more than those of a "naughty boy", even when they have been perpetrated on her. Mother appears to be firm with him and finds excuses for his behaviour and her treatment of him, in his father's treatment of him as a child. I do not feel that she is really determined to come to grips with her son's problem.

Ability Below average for his year.

Date 7th September,   1979   Signed   [signature]

So after a few telling off I put creative skills to good use and made a comic , Titan , it was an a4 sheet folded twice over and stapled to another , I did a comic strip highlighting the adventures of a space explorer , I coloured in all the characters , space ships and the aliens into the comic and sold them weekly for 10p , I sold quite a few but a friend Clive Manning has to get a mention as he thought of the baddies , which looked similar now to the cheap pop up aliens you see often with one eye .

Going off subject slightly (but going back on shortly)

(in later life When I was a catering manager in London at the premier of Monsters Inc the movie when I was in my late 20s I wanted to sue the film company Pixar as the alien with 1 eye(Mike wysoski) was a replica of the drawings I made when I was 11 , grrrr)

In my first year at Belvidere school a friend Neil threw a pencil at Mr Walsh, the geography teacher, Mr Walsh the gangly hippy turned sharply and pointed to me.

DRAAAAAYYYYYCOOOOOOT, GET HERE.

"No way Mr Walsh it was not me", he bounded towards me and virtually dragged me to the front of the class, he has a slipper which he wrote WOP on in chalk on the underside so when it hit your ass it would spell POW, you would have to wear it all day and if he collared you without it later you would get another WOP on the opposite buttock.

Seriously if I seen him today I would highly probably go up to him and do the same (I would probably get charged with assault.)

I lashed out at him when he tried to slipper me, I then accidently on purpose I hit him in the face with my clenched fist.

Off to Mr Revells to get the cane. Not once did I cry when being caned by Revell, always thinking I'm going to get you back one day you basterd (or probably thought, my dad is going to beat you up).

Again later in life When I was concierge to Bob Monkhouse the English comedian for the day in London 2000-ish , we were talking about when he was young you could count his friends on the fingers of captain cooks bad hand , just like Revell , no one apart from the jobs worthy teachers liked him .

Mr Bunce was a towering figure of a man who stood over me many times with a raised eyebrow and sometimes a shouty shouty voice and also Mr Cox our music teacher did not like me as I took the piss in every class I had with him, Mr Cox if your reading this I sincerely and truthfully apologise for being a little shit, I HAVE grown up and I HAVE really done something with my life.

I read in one police report 1979 that was I chased by a police officer who knew me, he chased me over a brook, behind the safeway food store, he chased me into a scrap yard (demolished salop car breakers), now replaced with a multi plex cinema, Chinese restaurant and expensive pub who serves crap food .

I got caught hiding with the box of bananas in a scrap car , which I refused to get out of saying you cannot arrest me in here unless you have a warrant , I remember him dragging me out of that car with no windows or boot , in fact it was a shell.

He said in a report to head master that he seen that I was carrying a box of bananas from the rear of the store and followed.

(A few friends found a hideout by the old gay meadow football ground in abbey Foregate, just down the road from safeways food store.

We used to go to this abandoned ww2 bunker which was on British rail property and take the booty we had stolen and either share it out or just eat it .

I stayed in the shelter a few times in my absconding days and the thing still stands and still has my name written on the ceilings, which we did in candle smoke (smoke turned black on the wall or ceiling if you held the candle close enough)

But Just my luck to be seen by a passing copper.

Children and young offenders act 1933, 20th June 1979

Theft and criminal damage, burglary

Oh dear , I remember this all too well and was very sorry to the courts that me and me ole mate Brian broke into Monkmoor girls school , drew on the walls with marker pen , paint etc , but mainly we got flour and eggs from the kitchen and had a jolly over the walls and floors , it was a real mess.

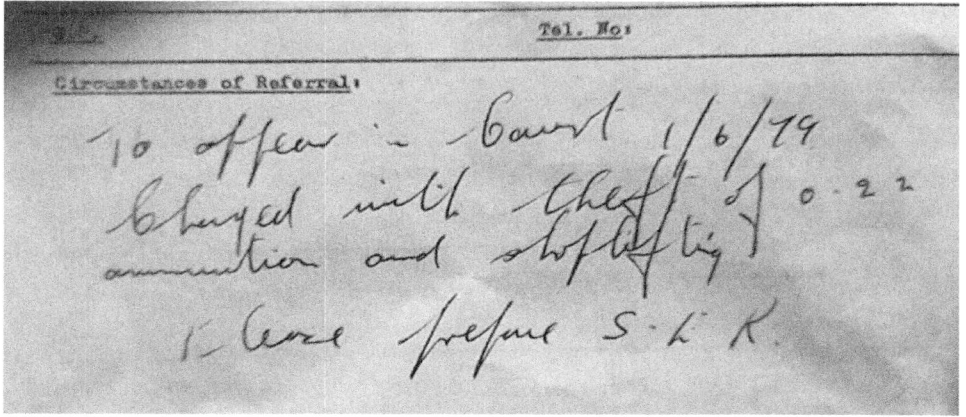

We got caught again, how, I do not know but front page news the following day.

School was closed for a week, I felt very guilty the following months about that.

For that you jointly with Brian break into Monkmoor girls school without lawful excuse and with the intention of causing damage , did cause damage to a window , books , furniture ,documents , books, eggs and a quantity of food stuffs belonging to Shropshire Education authority to the amount of £252,91.

For that you jointly with Brian break into Sankeys warehouse without lawful excuse and with the intention of causing damage, did cause damage by fire to the building causing £30,000 worth of damage.

12 counts of crime taken into consideration

That was a full one for the juvenile court to consider , all my past 3 months of stealing was about to be written off , I think I admitted to crimes I did not do , I just admitted them as the good cop , bad cop scenario led me to believe that nothing would happen to me if I admitted every crime that Shrewsbury had unsolved , I have on report a total of 6 boxes of banana's on different occasions in 1979 , imagine the nick name I would have been stuck with if the banana heists went in the paper , it would have stuck with me even to today .

(Just had a read through and I'm missing loads of Full stops, sorry about that)

23/04/79   Belvidere Boys school, Shrewsbury

Quite, unobtrusive, impresses as a cheerful lad willing and cooperative pupil.

Outside direct supervision he is deceitful and involves himself in petty crime of which there have been numerous instances throughout his first year and these have brought to light similar misbehaviour outside school.

Immature , devious by nature guileless expression totally misleading , he seems to have no conception of right and wrong as far as theft is concerned and in fact , would seem to be pre meditated , rather than opportunist, there seems to be no change in attitude over this term .

Signed. Mr Revell.

My grandmother had a fine stock of whiskey in the cellar , mini , 1L , 5L bottles and mini kegs , why she had these I do not know , I'm sure she didn't drink

She was divorced and going out with a lovely man called Wilf who me and my sister found dying on the floor in the kitchen in my nans large B&B, he had fallen off the back of the kitchen stool and was gasping for breath, we did not know what to do about this as we never encountered a heart attack before, we had a panic but instead of using the house phone we went down the road to the telephone box and dialled 999.

We were under strict orders not to use nans bright red dial phone for anything, so we didn't but I think I remember it having a mini lock on it due to the dossers who frequented the house for £2 per night, they mainly shared a dorm room but £3 got you a single, mum did the breakfast for the £8.00 B&B residents, I usually stole the whiskey sat on the roof and got drunk , considering I was a 4ft nothing fat ,spotty , ugly kid I felt like an adult when I did that (and doing that was too often) .

The ambulance peoples told my gran he may have survived if 10 mins earlier, to think it would have taken me and my sister that long to stop panicking and use the house phone.

Bless the man he was truly lovely xx.

The dossers who lived at the back of this large house where a funny bunch, I got to know a few of them and they all had character,

But most importantly they had money to buy little bottles of whiskey from me for half the price of Dot Allan's shop; I was destined to be in retail distribution (which funny enough was my first job during college)

Oh dear not again (I keep finding charge sheets muddled up in my reports

- Children's and young person's act 1933   04/05/1979.

Burglary & cycling offence – report to head regarding school record

Now I think to myself why oh why would they charge me for cycling over pavements and being chased by the police on a cycle when I just burgled the cycle shop in town , surely 1 charge would have been good enough but I think they wanted to throw the book at me .

Or pc [_____] wanted to , a 6ft towering gangly copper , fat face and child looking (and still is I presume and an inspector sergeant , I believe he gained a queens medal for his loyalty , he tried to blackmail me around 2010 by bringing me in the station , offer me a financial reward ? and to drop charges the reason being - a group of us were going to give testaments in court regarding an officer who seriously assaulted a lad walking up the road late at night by my house carrying a holdall, the lad was later acquitted and the officer reprimanded , as I had photo evidence as I was walking up the street to confront the officers assaulting this youth) Mr[_____]told me in a private interview a financial reward could be given out to me for information – meaning drop the charges and I will give you money , he also carried in the police interview room , every file on me dating from 1979 , it must have been nearly 2ft thick.

Why would you want to do that Mr[   ]?

I walked out and carried on with the charges, I don't like bent coppers, no loyalty.

I hope your reading this Mr [   ] you bent fucker.

I am currently pursuing this with ACRO (criminal records office) and the iopc (independent office for police conduct(but i really do not seeing me being here when the outcome arrives).

Latest laws are that I cannot complain about an officer if before Dec 2012, so I have to apply for freedom of information to gain the info or I will gain the police CCTV records to prove me to be correct on this.

Shrewsbury's Pc Brown had it in for me also around 1979/80 he was the main beat copper who was always looking for me and stopping me at every occasion he could, not hard when you live 200 yards from the cop shop and even closer to the main school, but we came to clash 6 years later when I got my first car, that ended badly for him?. (Explained later)

Detective Goodchild is one of the best officers I have ever had the pleasure to deal with at my young age, always treated me well

I have total respect for that man, I do believe he is now the community liaison officer for Shrewsbury, but I could be wrong.

My reports from early 1979 roughly go on to say roughly what the previous years have said , *childish , devious , but Mr. Revell has also added to my previous report .Immature , fails to respond to correction of minor childish behaviour , deceptively pleasant natured , lacking in self-esteem or drive*

I think it must be stressed that in recent months the incidents in which he has been involved have been in an irritating nature most of them arise out of his determination to create enjoyment for himself whatever the situation so that told one day of some infringement, he will be found doing precisely the same thing the following day, very untrustworthy.

40 days absent out of a possible 317 at school – poor report, recommendations made

I was charged 16 times for offences in 1979 whilst at Belvidere school at 12 1/2 yrs old.

Police liaison, inspector Jenks

On the 25th June 1979 , these 2 boys truanted from school and went to Woolworths and stole 2 cans of spray paint they then went to spray the walls between mother care and Woolworths until the containers were empty , when the containers were empty they then went in Halfords and stole 2 more cans , they then made their way to the multi-story car park and started to spray cars , while spraying their bikes they were apprehended by the car owner , Timothy ran away but was later picked up , both were interviewed in the presence of the parents and charged with causing £90 worth of damage . (This ended up being £15.00 on the final charge sheet)

The police will prosecute both boys.

Timothy Draycott, Abbots green, Monkmoor.

The late arrival of Timothy and his mother at court would seem to indicate the extent of their feelings towards Authority.

It is intended to commence a programme of intermediate treatment for timothy next month , run by a group of social workers for an anticipated period of 3 months , I have approached timothy in this connection , I have told him that I expect him to be involved .

I am certain that a greater degree of structure is needed if timothy is to benefit from supervision , Timothy has agreed to the proposal , this will take place at Monkmoor youth club premises and not his home , will prove effective – (Yeah right , let's see , TD)

Moving onto court January 1979.

For the offences June 1979 - supervision order 1 year, Dec 1979 - supervision order for 1 year, January 1980 supervision order 2 years (the care order came in June 1980)

Juvenile Court - 01/06/1979 , Theft , theft , theft , burglary , theft from clothes lines, burglary , criminal , damage , theft of bicycles , arson , criminal damage , more theft ,shoplifting , theft from vehicles , minor road traffic offence, etc .

15th January 1980 Juvenile court – (sentenced from Dec 1979)

Supervision order for 2 years, Compensation £20.04, Fines totalling £7.00

Chapter 3 – (the "Oh fuck me" chapter).

The 1980's was a very interesting decade for me , 1980 , 81 & 83 being the most memorable , I remember so well John Lennon getting shot , something about princess Diana ? , I think that is when bugger lugs Charles and Di got together (not researched)Interesting music as I was transgressing from punk to new wave music , Who shot J.R Ewing was a biggy and even I was engrossed in that more than that volcano erupting , The Falkland's war was just about to get underway which would lead to An acquaintance of mine going to prison for a long time for murder (Hilda Murrell) , personally I do not think he (Andy George) did it , we all believe it was political and to do with sinking of the general Belgrano , Andy was a nice lad who did a spot of burglary but always a gentle lad , but

My new Punk music love being from a night at the buttermarket warehouse (now a nightclub) when I was 12 and a bit, Colin Dickenson an old friend who also recently passed away put an illegal night on at the disused buttermarket with some others, we (myself, Clive manning, Karl Evans and his brother Dave) heard about this as both of them lived local to the club.

We went around and got confronted by a burly punk rocker who said we can come in if we spray the walls with cobweb spray, we happily agreed as we picked up cases of the stuff.

Karl had a 18" tall blonde Mohican , I had tramlines (which Karl forced upon me saying I looked like a fat little wimp with long wavy hair) , (my hair at the time tended to grow outwards so it looked like I had headphones on) so with short hair we looked the part anyway , Clive was just Clive with big floppy hair , we called him backbone as he walked lazy and hunched over , backbone meaning a Neanderthal style man .

It was all systems go in the completely empty shell of the buttermarket , bands setting up , lighting being bodged and greebo's everywhere , I remember them so well towering over me .

A hastily made bar selling tenants super and the bands tape recordings

I cannot remember too much of the night and the music though, but I was assured in later life that it was the angelic upstarts (not confirmed – just hearsay).

(We did follow it up with a sneak into the music hall in mid 81 (?) to see the Damned , I had run away from Besford house (my first care home a year later) just to see them but I thought as we stood just behind the large curtains at the sides ,aggh just remembered - April , it was April 1981 , near my sisters birthday .

I usually associate years with the music that was played and charted at the time, I would be fine on radio 2s popmasters on name the year.

1980 being boomtown rats (Crap) the who (Crap) but the Ramones , The specials ,the Beat & Blondie (to name only a few) I listened to mainly , simple minds came a year later .

On a regular bases we used Karl's Air rifle to shoot the windows of the Dana Prison ,(at the rear of Karl's house , we sat on his roof window) mainly shooting though the pears and plums from his mothers garden as we could hear the crack of the 177 pellet hitting the prison sewing room windows (I will know that room very well later in life) and on one occasion a prison warden was doing his local round around the prison when he shouted at us for throwing stones at the windows , I stuck the V up as we knew he could not leave his round , Mr Cox reminded me years later that it was him doing the rounds , he was a local man who seemed to know everyone (My mum included for visiting dad in earlier years).

Oh bugger me, where I was.

21/09/1979 – social report

Timothy is now living with his grandmother but has admitted to spraying the shop, car park and parked cars, he simply thinks he was enjoying himself, his sentence was deferred for 3 months.

11/10/79 - Mother has a definite lack of supervision in the family, mother blaming it on an abusive father.

20/10/79- Timothy seen at Mrs Norgroves (Gran) he was very upset because his mouse had died, this seemed like an infantile reaction.

18/12/79 –discussed with Timothy the upcoming court regarding the spray painting, bicycle shop theft, Burglary

28/12/79 – court date, Timothy did not arrive, adjourned

11/01/80 court date - supervision order for 2 years with 60 hours I.T. **(?)**

(No not I.T as in now's I.T , it was the I.T then in the 80s, don't ask me what it spells as I cannot be bothered to look , as I'm on a roll with the typing , me and my laptop are as one).

I discussed with timothy that if he fails to adhere to the supervision order he may well end up in care, I advised Timothy came in to discuss dates for the I.T to start.

24/01/80 – Timothy came into the office he arrived on a battered bike, I told him he would need to get this fixed as he could be charged by an officer or could cause an accident.

Timothy is expected to attend his first I.T on the 07/02/80.

Timothy arrived at I.T at Monkmoor Youth club,

15-17 Feb 1980, we went to a cottage for the weekend in Minstrelsy, Timothy was well behaved and enjoyed the outing, I.T will continue for a while with no upsets.

We went to Blist hill museum, Acton Scott working farm, the safari park and many more

I really do not remember any of these outings at all but I must have been to them as they are all written here next to me.

35 years later I would be catering with my own company at all of those mentioned venues.

I.T was going well in the first 3 months the reports state, my father was berating me and it shows in the social all reports from Feb- April reports, mother was settling in well now her (other) abusive boyfriend Richie (since past away the wife beating c**t) was off the scene.

30/04/80, Timothy was not very communicative as his father had given him a large flea in his ear the night before Mr Draycott is playing an active part in the family now and supporting Mrs Draycott in some ways, they all agree that Richie is not welcome anymore.

Brother Tony is due home from Quinta School in Weston rhyn, near Oswestry in early June.

(That place also had Historic Sexual abuse claims – but that's not my story).

04/06/80 – *Visited Mrs Draycott in relation to tony being allowed home from Quinta and to discuss the court date with Timothy, Mrs. Draycott Defends timothy saying he was easily led, but timothy had admitted to breaking into the bike shop and the school after I spoke to him alone, it was brians idea to set fire to the polystyrene in the warehouse causing over £30,000 damage.*

Tim feels no remorse for his actions, knowing he has done wrong but saying he liked throwing food and going on adventures. (!)

Discussed a potential care order with Tim and he did not seem concerned as he thinks he may be going to the mount in wellington as Brian was there already and quite a few other lads he knew from school .

Tony is trying to be a role model for Tim now he I released, Tony seems to be adjusting very well to being home and is looking for a job.

Discussed with Tim the other offence he has just committed on the night of my last visit , breaking into a cycle shop for a speedometer , I had a long talk with Tim about this and the stupidity of it when a court date has been set for the other offences .

He apparently seemed not bothered, but then a lot worried when I mentioned the implications of a care order.

I think he's beginning to realise the seriousness of what he has done.

Discussed with the Head Mr Howells that Tim could benefit from a residential care order in the right settings, we discussed about placement at the Mount

(Shropshire Council should have stuck to that, you bastards, more about the Mount later)

Visited Mrs Draycott to discuss the possible outcome at court , she was upset that she would not see Timothy until he was 18 , Just like his brother and that Tim was only a baby , she disapproves of care and sees it as repressive rather than a form of help , I explained to Mrs Draycott that it may help but she feels he is too young for care and what they may do to him (me)

How correct you were mother

I was placed in care at Besford house 30th June 1980 due to the criminal damages the previous year on the Sankeys warehouse at £30,000 damage (so much money back then & even now) and the cycle shop, this was a home known to many in Shrewsbury as a naughty boys and girls home .

To the Court from social services.

On 1st June timothy was made the subject of a supervision order which was disappointing.

He began the intermediate programme for 10 sessions and a weekend away, he did not emerge as a troublemaker or ringleader

my care officer at the time Mr Carson took me to Besford after being placed on the care order on the 27th June , I remember sitting next to him (no seatbelts on)in his 1970s Vauxhall viva driving up a car crowded thin street (I would later steal at least 20 of those cars in the next 2 years) .

 Turning from Trinity Street into the drive of the 1800s house, quite dominating white coloured building, loads of windows at the front, it looked like the Addams family house I was literally shitting myself.

But I was promised enroute that I would get a garden plot (which I got) , this due to the fact of me helping my nans boyfriend Wilf pot up the geraniums for the flower show display .

The house was built in 1893 as a private residence and then in 1911 turned into a boy's home to free up the workhouses, social services took over in the 1960s.

 I remember shaking uncontrollably (something that would stay for me for years when I was nervous) and Mrs Warring in her office and her soothing voice saying I was going to love it , all the activities I will be going on in the holidays , all the new children I will meet , IT WILL BE GREAT , she said....

Mother had been given a house by my grandmothers just up the road from my grans house in the posh-is side of town on the Abbey Foregate on the main road, a lovely sticky out small Victorian house, father was in new park close but jumping from working in Holland and back again, well away from the family and a bonus I was just a mile away in Besford, home at weekends, everything was rosy.

I still walked to school from Besford house, past my grans house (which I used to pop in many times on the way back, Besford seemed ok with this until I started to get in trouble again with a lad called Tony Simcoe (Dodd).

He took his own life when he was 18, dumped by a local girl he loved so much, he drove down to Weston super mare, placed a pipe from the exhaust to car and killed himself, I feel sometimes I have to copy that as he would have thought of the easiest way to do what he did, the man was very calculated, he seemed to see problems and planned whilst in my company, and I will tell you all about our country wide antics shortly.

He was 2 years my senior and was placed in Besford a few weeks after I arrived, we hit it off quite well as he was from out of town, a majority of the children in the home being from inside the town and me being a loner I did not want to mingle with the locals, Tony had pitted skin, looked rough all the time, 2ft taller than podgy me, his attitude was the same as mine, so we hit it off as friends for years to come.

Police liaison letter on file 29/07/80.

Timothy took a cycle worth £80 and gave it to Mr Dodd, Draycott denies this.

1 month later the police saw the boys on some cycles, after inspecting the cycles it was proved to be the stolen cycle

Charged - Juvenile court – July 28th 1980

That you did with another steal a Raleigh solitaire pedal cycle worth £80.00

And jointly with another enter a building with the intention to steal a viscount pedal cycle worth £64.00.

Little did they know we were out robbing a lot more than bikes, I introduced Tony to all the others in the home, I told him to avoid some care workers which looked after us as one of them MR A was constantly making lewd comments at me, I now realise in later life that this was called grooming but we didn't have groomers then we just had pervs, I don't even think we used the word peado.

(I do believe Mr A was later accused for crimes at the home by another pupil, I read in the Shropshire star in the mid nineties, name of the abused lad escapes me but I really wanted to back him up, I really could not as this would expose me for being in a naughty boys home when at the time I had a high up job in London when all this news broke out. (Internet was not really around then)

I do not think nothing happened regarding that case , he highlighted it enough in the papers , I do not think it went to court , if your reading this (abused lad) I will now back you up on the names of the abusers if anything comes about from this memoir .

If your reading this Mr A , (quite a young man around 30 at that time , straight on top but wavy brown hair on the sides , young face), Read on Mr A as you are mentioned numerous times and so you know it's you I am going to mention your name subliminally.

First few weeks in Besford were a nightmare.

I was fresh faced so Mr A trying it on with me in spoken word to start , then when I started to get into trouble more at school , constantly touching me on my ass or front packet when in passing .

I remember me and Tony absconding to his aunt's house in Northampton when Mr A touched me for the first time only a few weeks after I arrived at Besford, the first week or so Tony was at Besford.

We walked the tracks to wellington whence we stole a fiesta mk1, (take the quarter light window out with a penny, rip off the steering wheel ignition cover, place a small bar over the barrel and break off, you can then start it with a penny or suchlike) we drove all the way to Northampton without batting an eyelid (I was passenger).

Some of the best times in my life (at that time) happened around these months.

Now going back a bit to 11/01/1980 but court date was July 1980.

"Come on" shouted the copper "we know you are in here, we have dogs and we will use them "

Oh fuck , here is me Brian (run away from the mount home wellington)and martin Laine (since tragically died in a motorcycle accident) inside the new market hall in Shrewsbury separated from each other as the market hall had cubicles for traders to deal from .

Our plan (which was working so far)was to stay in the furniture shops furniture and sneak out late at night to rob each cubicle of its booty , so far so good , it was approx 9pm and the place was empty and dead .

We stayed together for Midda's clothes shop and wore the leather jackets we took but knowing Midda they would have been cheap imitation knock offs (Midda being a towering 6.5" Indian man who my mother got on with well when buying our school clothes , come on - everyone in the county in the 80s shopped at Midda in the market.

We then jumped from cubicle to cubicle in the market hall until we got to the Jewellery, we had a field day filling our new jackets with what we thought was gold, we then decided to split up to get things done quicker.

Just as a copper bellowed out his orders saying " the place was surrounded" our heads popped up over the balcony cubicles , we saw each other but the copper down on the ground floor could not see us , we all nodded to each other to make our way to the far end of the market balcony .

I made it to the end of the market hall alone and started to climb up over some security grills they pull down to close the market hall , over the mechanism , then down the other side making me then outside the building , as I was going down , martin I could see was going up and over whilst I was looking directly at the copper through the grill , it seemed like forever looking at him , I knew he couldn't get me , the area was clear behind me of coppers so I just casually went down the security grill , knowing they must have been the other side of the market hall 100 yards away , Ha , GOT YA .

I started to run towards the river, Blokes outside the exchange pub laughing at us running up the hill next to them, by what they were saying they knew exactly what was going on, I just don't recall what they were saying?

Myself and martin made it to our bikes, Brian got caught and we got caught the following day, we dumped all booty whilst fast peddling away along the river.

Myself , Brian and Martin also stole a car in Shrewsbury and took it for a joy ride to find other cars and ended up in a town not so far away , the most desirable of cars were about to be stolen after we broke into the car showroom shop , all used cars

A Sierra Cosworth , a display model MG Metro but the rally version , the name escapes me but it was something like the r467 blah blah or something , the police chase which came about ended up with us hiding under an old bridge and the police like idiots speeding past us with blue lights on . (Into the bat cave – not as glamorous though near Market Drayton)

It was surreal at the time as we knew about this abandoned bridge with ivy growing at the front and a track leading 50 yards from the main rd to the disused rail bridge

We seen them lights from 5 miles away, I often wonder why they keep their blue lights on when nearing a burglary in progress, especially up a straight?

The night we did this was not long after the market hall heist (sorry - failed heist)

Myself and a person who does not want to be named as I was the only one caught entered WhSmiths in town through a back way down a place we call the 70 steps in Shrewsbury Town centre, steps leading from the top of the town (the hill) to the bottom of town (not on the hill), I don't even think there were 70 steps, I'm sure 68, but I'm sure I will get rectified.

It was a difficult place to get into but we were confident that we could do it , it took a couple of large brick walls to clamber over , a drain pipe to scale and some barbed wire to get over , it was a proper colditz to get in but we managed it .

We entered in the bottom floor and were careful not to trigger any door alarms; we were very noticeable on the other side of the door if you looked in from the town centre main road.

We went through a door not alarmed and proceeded to steal the Casio calculator watches and posh parker pens (with nibs), nothing else really worth stealing, on our way out my friend accidently closed a door which we had fixed open, this enabled the alarms to start straight away, really weird but as we was going through another door we noticed a copper with a torch at the front looking in , this meaning they were alerted before the alarms went off (good lesson learnt for the future ?), oh shit time to get our skates on.

We managed to get to the 70 (68) steps and down to the bottom without getting caught but then straight into the arms of a copper at the bottom of the steps about to go up the steps.

I'm beginning to think I'm not very good at this burglary stuff so I stopped about then, I do mention a couple more in the book later on which had to be done in desperation.

Summer 1980 was also memorable in the sense my charge sheets says so.

Oh the horse, we stole a horse. Time out, Time out, got to mention this..

I took the horse with lainey on 14th February 1980, I do not remember to much apart we vere tipsy (probably on nans whiskey and we fell in love with it on this memorable night) and ended up with a horse 2 miles down an old canal track, I think looking at the location we were at the base of a local hill at Haughmond along the old canal from Shrewsbury.

Report states the horse was given to the adjoining house and we were given a lift home, sorry- that story didn't go far.

I was going to place all my charge sheets here for the months from January 1980- July 1980 but my word does it take up a lot of space and Giga Bytes if you're reading this on kindle.

I really hate to say this but my crimes for them months was 28 , that is disgusting I'm breaking it down now to 4 per month , that's 1 per week , that's disgusting considering what I was doing at that age (13 yr old).

I don't want to but to name a few which I took into consideration, Owen , Owen , (I went around that town shop in 4 hours) , Boots , Music hall , Belvidere pub ,nearly all the shops in Abbey Foregate + more , many more .

Right let's get them bad memories out of my head and let's get onto the crime spree from July 1980, I'm not really looking forward to writing this either.

Oh my I've just spent quite a few days of reading on the next items I am about to write about , it's just getting worse and beginning to upset me to think of the hurt I must have caused people during these years , me crying is an understatement at the moment , this book has definitely effected my mental health over the past few weeks that I have to give time out for a few weeks , sorry , hey wait a moment why am I apologising you only have to read on , der

Chapter, I've lost count, so let's just carry on without chapters for the time being.

By reading my reports I think by this time care home , home and school are getting to either know Me better or what I thought was picking on me due to me being easily led, (that's what my mum said – easily led)

In June /July 1980 I burgled , got caught for being the instigator in these crimes (amongst others) a Fishing tackle shop , another chip shop , 2 pubs , the Quarry flower show office , The swimming baths , the Pengwern boat club – twice , Shrewsbury town football club break and entering – twice , 2 criminal damages , 2 shoplifting , 3 juvenile court dates in 3 months = another care order , mum said I was easily led ?

Sorry , I have to take time out to tell you about the football club its silly , it's not a crime I regret as I have been to see Shrewsbury town FC in later life many times (I've paid my dues), including 2 Wembley final league play offs and they have always fuckin lost , in fact the only winner I have seen in a Shrewsbury stadium was Elton john in concert , ha stick that up your arse STFC , (I still support you though by buying a mug every year)

So ... me and a mate decided on the Shrewsbury town football club , (Gay meadow , Abbey Foregate ,Shrewsbury) easy to get in , easy to rob the shop (just slide the window) , it was a football night as we thought we would get more and they might leave the money in the till .

So on the secondary school side (now a college or they like to call it a sixth form college). We scaled the wall and preceded to the club tuck shop (pie and chips etc) en-route my friend found a Scottish £20 note on the floor – Bonus.

(Sorry, going back a paragraph, I buy a STFC mug every few years – Not every year)

We entered the club shop, some pies still warm in the hot cupboard and wow the till had money in it around £45 so we were definitely up on the day, we grabbed the mars bars and Twix's, boxes this time, we placed these in the crisp boxes stuffed full of cheese and onion and ready salted, as that all they sold and a few cold sausage rolls (that's all they sold on every item).

We thought we would put these by the escape wall and go see if the club house was open.

Bonus – the doors to the whole football club were open and we went straight into the changing rooms of both sides , Shrewsbury's all messy , they did not clean up after the game , the away side was mint clean .

We got to the front clubhouse through some offices, always on guard but why cars still out the front? , we brushed it off and carried on filling bags full of Shrewsbury town tops , caps , badges etc , a car pulled up right outside the shop , we ducked down and started to inch our way towards the back door , we were crouching along the corridor so not to be seen and came up to the pitch , we sprinted towards the escape wall with shouting from every angle , looking around I seen loads of people with bin bags cleaning around the ground standing area , where the hell did they come from ? .

One started to run at us but as I was going over the goal post supporters wall he tripped up, I think quite badly as he didn't seem to get up as I was going over the (3ft) wall.

We dropped loads of stuff clambering up a advertising post to get to the top of the school wall (20ft), we didn't get the mars bars or Twix but what we did get was a Scottish £20 note which I did not get to see, the money we spent on whatever was popular at the time I suppose, I cannot recall.

I often think to myself was I either an easy touch for these house masters through the times I was at care or did I give off signals for fully grown men to try it on with me , I really do not think so as I touched my first girlfriend at 11 making me heterosexual surely ?.

The big shed at Besford, wow that was a big shed, Besford kept its stock and also a recreational area with table tennis, pub games and such like.

(I distinctly remember the Corona pop stacked up in crates just inside the doorway on the right as I used to steal the empty bottles through the broken window and get 5p from Dot Allen's shop in Monkmoor road for the empty bottle)

The big green (football, rugby field) outside the back of Besford was surrounded by thick set bushes and trees, hiding the houses beyond the 6ft wall

The Wooden shed (approx 30m x 12m) was also the bordello of Mr A and Mr B at different times of the year; I don't think they knew that the other was also an abuser. (But I could be wrong) I can say they didn't try it with me together but pupils have told me in later life that Mr B knew Mr A was doing it. (Mr B was much older)

I really wish I could describe them properly but apparently I am not allowed unless I now press charges, prosecute or whatever has to be done, I'm not ready to do that yet.

Julie was a local friend of mine in Besford, she also moved to the vineyard juvenile assessment centre in 81 when I was also assessed there.

I don't remember speaking to her at Besford about this (but she told me a few years later at the vineyards home) about Mr B coming up to me and saying that he needed a hand in the shed putting things away, apparently I followed him and he tried it on by grabbing me and trying to kiss me, Julie told me that I was hysterical when speaking to her.

Fat, sweaty, hideous man, but who reminded me of the Frankie Howard acting in up Pompeii, (Sorry Frankie Howard was not fat)

He touched, rubbed, and groped, everything he could do to get a reaction from me.

"Cum on me lover, giss us a little peck on the cheek me boy lover, cum on, no one will know"

(The amount of times I will quote that line in this book – "No one will know")

(Ha, just proofed read this myself and found that I only mention it twice – Bonus)

(Yes, you know who you are, read on Mr B)

Maybe Julie was mixed up, when I remember when he tried it on with me for the first time, I remember so well, it's drilled in my brain and gets brought up very often in my thoughts.

I had a hideout by the old gay meadow football club, I still used to go to , that was my sanctuary and had been since I was 9-10 years old , an old Air raid shelter , which is still standing and still with my name in the ceiling in candle smoke writing .

Some friends back in 80/81 wrote "oh he's pissed again" on the walls in relation to my bed wetting whilst camping out with them (Karl , I will never forget it)

It was sung on the back drop of Phil Collins he's missed again which were early 81 I think.

Enough of all that, that song rings in my head virtually every week, let's crack on with my story and my regrets.

26th November 1980. (That's the exact date, proven in the files) 5PM -7PM

Just got back from school around 4pm, as usual tony Simcoe (Dodd) and me starting playing, at that time it was Bodie and Doyle from the professionals TV programme.

My gran brought me a plastic kit of a plastic gun, badges, spy glass, binoculars (didn't work) and handcuffs you could snap out of. (We also had an ID badge each).

And thinking to my files 2 years later my head master Mr Revell says that I should stop these silly tag style games.

We usually did a hide and seek around Besford, the bushes being the best place behind the wooden shed as it was so over grown, staff did not like us running around the main house.

On this occasion Tony hid in the back laundry room as I hunted , Mr B also was present and passing me when I was looking always making his sly comments about hiding with me ,even at that age I think I knew exactly what he was trying to do.

I was looking in my favourite places when the sweaty fat twat came up from the back bushes , grabbed me around the waste ,(I considered myself a fat strapping little lad then , coming in at 4.6" which is pretty hefty for an 12 1/2 yr old) and took me around the waist into the tree area , not so hidden away , slammed me against a tree and said something like " I have no time today , I'm on tomorrow , I have seen you and tony are very close and I want to be close as well so tomorrow with you and we can be closer , but then he touched me on my pecker. Cock, dick, member, call it what you like but at that age it was a pecker.

(Some say the name of it and size of it proves with age – not researched)

Then his hand went down, actually went down my jeans inside my pants and he started to grope.

That was too much; I have learnt a lesson in life from my father if anything was wrong, and so I stamped on his toe.

As I was struggling free he said again and again about the following night in the shed.

I could say it now in his accent and think of his face saying it, it's a disgusting thought

Now this is the man (sweaty twat) I seen standing upright in the shed a few weeks before getting a blowjob by a pupil my age, this is the man who spent a few weeks with me talking about my behavioural problems, I heard other stories from other pupils, I remember the names of at least half of the pupils at Besford in 1980-82, how could I ever forget them, I know the names of 3 that were abused at Besford house. I witnessed 2 get abused.

(The Mount home in Wellington being worse – I will come to that later after I now stop thinking about it, time for me to grab the Marlboro lights and rest my already stewed head)

I told people at the time , older friends of mine (friends , older brothers etc), I told this to my grandmother and if I remember correctly also the shop keeper , who knew me very well , she was a very wise lady, some staff I got along with at belvidere school , nearly all the pupils at Besford and when I went to be assessed a few weeks later at the Vineyards , Telford , I cried and cried about what was going on , but I see not one word written about it now in the vineyards files about me , even though I have all the reports (the councils have omitted many parts , blanked off – third party information they say).

And it would not surprise me to see them take pages away to be destroyed as I remember many things not mentioned in my reports which should have been mentioned.

I did not tell any member of my family as we were a dysfunctional family, not really close at all.

I told Tony Dodd when I found him about what B had just said and done in the back bushes.

He wanted to grab a rounder's bat and smash his face in , I was crying to much I think I wanted to but said let's just go , go we did .

I robbed the office of Besford house at around 4-5pm and managed to get roughly £35.00.
(We blagged Mr Cotterall the head master type bloke that a pupil has beer in his room).

Mr Cotterall went off on his jolly thinking we have turned over a new leaf by dobbing in a lad, Tony following Mr Cotterall.

We arranged to meet by the front gate if successful and if not I would be having tea with everyone else so I Went to the front of the house and started pushing up the large office sash window from the outside very easy as it on ground floor and right next to the main

Front door, I was on the other side of the large window so I could see anyone coming out of the front door through the bay window, any staff appearing I could then just duck down.

 (Text book burglary at that age, Ronnie Biggs would have been proud of me).

All others in the home getting ready to settle down after school and before tea or doing some recreation on the back lawn.

We decided when we met up that was enough money for us to get to as far away as possible.

We started off by stealing a Austin allegro Tony said he knew the old man kept his keys in the car but in his garage, his garage separated by at least 5 house's, I don't actually remember stealing it, actually driving it away, I do remember the asbestos corrugated roof we broke through, I remember me driving it or trying to and tony shouting at me and moving the gears for me , bloody nightmare but we ended up the road at crewe train station and getting on one of the last trains north.

Then around 6/7 hours later we ended up at Central station , Glasgow , very dominating indeed , we were a bit terrified of this place , it was dirty ,and smelly , even though we have ran away a few times to other towns , this was new to us , this was a BIG train station .

We avoided the police a couple of times who were lingering around the station , got loads of looks from people which probably put me on the paranoid trip , wow , what shall we do .

Well I need a wee; we had to get away from this busy place as we thought the police were looking at us, I see now why, 12 and 14 yr olds at 1/2am-ish in a busy train station – Not speaking the lingo.

We left through the main doors and turned left to go up a small bank, no luggage

I seen the large STV , (Scottish TV station building) and got quite excited by it , it was a big building , why I got excited I really do not know , but I did .

A public toilet was over the road so I told tony I was running over to the Lav.

Having a wee in this 1940s style toilet, a bloke walks up next to me," ar-right lad", he looked down at me nodding towards his cock shaking it and my little dick, I stared back up at him, winkled my willy and ran as fast as I could out the door, told tony, he got angry and we both started towards the toilet.

The 6ft-ish ragged tramp like bloke came out of the toilets and looked at us and started to walk up the bank looking back at us following him, why follow him I do not know but I know we gave in a few hundred yards, bloody pervert, do I just attract them with my young round cute face, TWICE IN 2 DAYS.

Well what do we do now, we were scared, had no money apart from a couple of pounds,

We phoned Besford on the thought they would come and get us straight away in the minibus but hoooo no as we were waiting for them in the train station (in the light)we were nabbed by 4 burly Scottish officers of the law .

We could not understand a word they were saying , we sat in the middle of battered up Leyland van with the burley coppers laughing at us and talking about Shrewsbury town being near London , and do we know so and so in London .

t would not be the first time in Scotland but I wet myself and I remember it running down my leg onto the floor of the black Mariah van, to scared to tell the haggis Gestapo sitting opposite us.

They took us to the police station, placed us in a room with large window on the wall.

 won't beat around the bush, glamorise it or anything.

2 coppers brought in a lad into that room next to ours, we seen them place him on a chair, ook towards us, we speculated later if it was a one way mirror.

We thought and maybe said, here is the bad cop, good cop scenario

They sat him down and they started to beat him, he was approx 18-25, he fell of his chair and they beat him some more, he was doubled up on the floor and we were as far away from that glass as we could be, wow, this is going to happen to us next, I wet the spare shorts the police gave me at the station.

2 coppers came in mid beating and looked at what was happening , told us to gather up our stuff and follow , they placed us in a car , handcuffs and at around 3am in the morning .

They drove a fair few miles to a place called Larch grove (not researched) , I woke tony in the back of the car when we got to the prison walls , yes , that's what I said ..Prison walls.

They handed us over to 2 wardens at the gate , they did not say a lot just took us to a room give us fresh clothes that fit , bed sheets , boots ,toiletries .

 don't remember conversations with them or with tony , but I do remember the layout of the prison , the bedroom dorm (8 in my dorm), courtyard , main office ,even down to the swathes of roses adjoining the main road leading out .

Morning came with banging from the screws on our metal framed tubular beds at around 7am.

The Scottish inmates could not speak to me at night as it was dark , the screws did not put any lights on , just directed me to the bed near the door , tony was placed in another room

What a weird morning this would be, as soon as I got up I was questioned by loads of lads older than me (16+), I could not understand a word of what they said, I did manage to get a few words out on where I am from, no one at all knew where Shrewsbury was so I had to explain to many but mainly they wanted to know what football league we are in.

Everyone was frogmarched to the showers where the screw directed me to a singular shower and stood outside the half door.

I met up with tony at the breakfast dining room, we where stared at from the minute we go in the canteen from every angle, we were the talk of the Scottish version of Borstal.

Breakfast was slop, (typical) porridge, maybe it was nerves or the amount of Scottish lads speaking to us but we did not eat, they ate it for us.

Why they made it a Scottish national food I do not know , it probably tastes like wall paper paste , sorry – I'm a hypocrite I'm looking left to see a box of Quakers strawberry oats on m kitchen shelf , never been opened , I felt obliged to buy it at home bargains as it was 50% off.

Just checked, out of date 2 months ago, that was a waste of money.

I was approached by a screw who informed me in his weird language and in front of 30-ish Inmates on my table that I had wet the bed and I need to go back now and take the sheets off

It went around the dining room in seconds, half the hall wailing and pointing at me   , taking the piss, I really do not know what was said but I'm sure it was not nice.

He (the caber tossing giant screw) led us to the dorm room, I did what he said by changing the sheets & blankets and throwing them in the laundry basket at the end of the corridor.

He then took us to a class room half filled with lads and the nicest old lady who taught me and tony how to weave baskets, we weaved a couple of small plant pot baskets before we were ushered away (she let us have the baskets for a pound each, they said all inmates pay for what they take home, a fuckin pound, that could get me half way across the country, leaving us with about 70p each of the stolen money).

A Social worker picked us up the following day and took us back to Besford , lecture after lecture for a 5 hour journey , We did not plan on escaping again while journeying down , bu I know it was quiet , no jolliness like on the way up to Glasgow .

Mr Cotterall (our principal at Besford) was not a happy man when we returned to Besford; we got picked up by Mr Pugh (My) social worker at the time.

He was a nice man .always wanted to talk about the problems we are having, did not shout, did not judge, and if you told him something it would be in confidence.

So shock and horror

I did on one occasion tell him and he told me to be quite about things like that but he would mention it, he obviously didn't or maybe he did, but no reports on this and I have viewed them many times.

Lucky for me Mr A was not seen for a while and I do not see his name on any of my reports until another 4 months later, in Dec 1980, I'm sure we will get to the later.

Mr B on the other hand was present, I think tony at the age of 14 gave him a warning as a few days later whilst walking up the corridor I was given a massive slap around the head from behind, that hurt and hurt a lot, I doubled up but got held up by Mr B, he gripped my collar bone so much to keep me upright "wanker, cunt, little shit, it all came out of his mouth in a forceful whisper. " I told you not to tell anyone, simcoe (Tony Dodd) will be shipped out soon and you will have no one to cry to".

I was apologising about it as he was about to clout me again, then he was soothing and started to promise me things, outings, a better room on my own.

Do we understand each other, I had to agree, his hand stayed massively gripped on my shoulder until he walked away.

Do not tell anyone, do not tell anyone, I was drilling in my head the words from that dirty smelly bastard.

That evening me and tony ran away.

We ended up going around town, no CCTV camera's then to keep an eye on us we ended up in the town walls church early evening.

A massive church I remember frequenting only during midnight mass at Christmas with a catholic friend.

I'm sure if he reads this he will be fuming as to what we did next, 2 oversized and overweight church charity boxes went over the 30ft town walls outside the church onto the allotments pavement below.

The 100 or so candles in holders that were welded on the 6ft charity boxes went with them.

1 smashed open; the other didn't but did come dislodged from the candle holder.

We ran around the road, down the bank, through some gardens to the allotments to pick up our booty.

We had to decide and decide quickly as I really did not want to go back to Mr B but we decided lets go to my grandmothers as she has loads of places to hide in the house.

We ended up in the cellar and heard the usual knocks on the door by the police to see if we were there, Nan had old Victorian vents in the walls and you could hear every word, the vents came in use many times in the 80's.

We found a tent? So decided that the following morning we should escape with our £6.85

From the church but very confident that the other box unopened would give us more.

We just needed to get away from Shrewsbury to try to open it; we jumped a train with some tinned food stolen from grans house, a tent and a holdall carrying a very jangling metal box.

We ended up in Coventry, what an eye opener for me seeing a life size model of a 6ft Indian Mary holding an Indian baby Jesus in a shop window down the high street, for years and years to come that puzzled me a great deal, and in a weird way still does.

Shrewsbury at the time was filled with racism , the EBF (English Border Front) were the local err how do we say this" Defenders " who defended our football supporters from defending other defenders of other defending teams , mainly from multi racial towns (does that make sense Mr. or Mrs. proof reader ?) , you would not see a lot of black or Indian nationals in Shrewsbury in the early eighties , a very white conservative town at the time .

We hid our booty in some bushes in the Coventry park while we went for a jolly to shoplift a tin opener , we ended up being chased by a shopkeeper for Tony stealing a chocolate bar (How petty).

We ended walking away with a camping stove, tin opener, toffee hammer? , mini crowbar and a electric kettle that looked like a stove top kettle , to name but a few , tony just happened to walk out of the store with , amazing .

I am sure we would have found an electric socket for the kettle.

It was dark when we returned to the booty in the bushes and as no lights on in the field we decided to pitch up tent there, oh what silly little persons we must have been.

We awoke to dog walkers and kids our age going to school walking past us.

We only picked the main park in the town to camp in, and right next to the main gate.

We started to pack away as quick as we could at 8-9am, but before we could pack the tent away 2 boys in blue decided to come have a look at us and unfortunately had a look in the tent to see a metal locked box and new boxed kitchen items.

Oh dear back to Besford without even getting out of the midlands.

Mrs Waring my social worker was not too pleased according to my reports she lectured me about the problems I have caused with my family and for letting down the abusers at Besford – Oops , sorry I was supposed to say carers then instead of abusers ., I'm sure my proof reader will also rectify that one as well .

Same old , same old , I had heard this lecture so many times from courts , carers , parents & Friends .

(Oh, police declared £3.11 in the Coventry Charity Box)

You tend to close your ears when they start to rabble on, I have learnt a very big lesson since then in listening to people and never ever talk over anyone mid conversation.

(In early life that would have been a clout around the head)

Never speak when spoken to, but most important never put your elbows on the table whilst eating, it still annoys me to this day, why I really do not know.

It was not to long (4 days) before I absconded again but this time with another lad after getting the cane again by Mr Revell for stealing a bicycle from school , apparently I was seen taking the bike from the bike sheds and casually riding out of the school at lunch time .

(I also stole a jacket, trainers, a holdall, a lad's lunch).

That's news to me, I really do not remember that but I really suppose my social worker would not lie about such things.

As Mr Revell had to tell Besford about my antics, I could not delay my departure, I went back to Besford and grabbed a few things before my key worker arrived and got the message about my stealing.

I asked tony if he wanted to come but he declined saying he had to behave or he would be taken to another boy's home.

I met up with Brian and we took his dads car from his garage (Morris ital), Brian could drive and I was still learning, but I knew the basics.

We went up to Haughmond and drove around abit; he started to get brave and started to drive faster.

It was not to long before we crashed through a farmer's large wooden gate. Which was stupidly placed on an L shaped bend.

On the left of the gate by 20ft was an electric pylon and on the right of the gate by 10 foot was an oil tank in the farmer's yard.

What a daft place to put that , the gate was totalled , the car was a total right off , windows smashed , bumpers off , crimpled basically , we were in shock but stunned this could happen .

Then we had the farmer next to us at 1am yelling at us but also caring words about our welfare.

The police were called so that meant another court date; I remember later going back and fixing the gate and doing some menial work for the farmer.

Brian's dad not so pleased wrote off his car and I got the blame for leading him astray.

That was the first of many cars to the extent that I was classed later as the most prolific car thief in Shrewsbury. (Along with Martin Laine who a few years ago passed away in a motorcycle accident and of course Brian who would later be my partner in crime but later I would hate him for grassing me up burgling the market hall in Shrewsbury (I will tell you later on about that adventure).

Life was about to change for me now I knew the basics of a car.

My First car theft came very shortly after I got the cane from Mr Revell for stealing Milk and fresh orange juice from a doorstep and stupidly taking it into school , Revell seeing me walking into school with them in doorstep bottles , he knew we were on milk tokens and mother gave them us to give the school weekly .

It was the day of that cane that made me go straight after school to my football ground hideout car park , smashed the back quarter light window to the new-ish green ford escort , ripped the barrel of with a brick and used the customary penny piece to turn the ignition , we advanced to ripping the barrels off with a 2ft scaffolding bars soon after , which we kept at various places around town , every opportunity to steal a scaffold pole was taken , not just by me but a few others and we shared where we hid them .

I went to pick up Clive who also went to Belvedere and was easily led, he got scared so I let him out of the car and picked up Brian.

He wanted to drive so I agreed until we got out of town, he decided to take the through town route to get to the Telford road instead of going the long way around haugmond hill.

Upon approaching the railway station a cop car came along side us asking us to pull over , obviously Brian did not want to do this and carried straight on up town while the copper got cut up on the road , forcing him to stop hard , we approached the top end of town and as coming around a sharpish corner pretty fast on a hill we were confronted with a copper waving his arms in the middle of the road , Brian did not care he drove straight at the copper , he dived out of the way saying later he had grazes to the legs .

Brian sped off through the top of town until we came to a large steep bank leading out of town called the Wyle cop , it was on a very sharp bend and Brian did not take it correctly , we ended up going down the steep bank side ways , this very steep bank and going down side ways was not a funny experience , we ended up wedged in a lamp post half way down outside a pub called the nags head , I was trapped in my seat as the post had imbedded in my door , I looked around to see Brian high tailing it down the road .

That boy could run, always said it and so did the coppers who could never ever catch him.

He would have made it big in Olympic running.

Well the obvious happened , the police car caught up whilst I was still in shock and trying to clamber out of the driver's side , pinned to the ground by cop 1 and 2 while cop 3 went in the car to catch Brian (they got him the next day).

Mr B was still up to his old tricks with me , always the comments about we will soon be together but luckily no touching , these comments were enough to make me stay away from Besford as much as I could , this carried on for a few weeks as I absconded a few times more in this duration , but it made me quizzical about the no touching at that time , maybe he was content with another lad who I didn't speak to much , so we shall call him Simon (name changed) , I do know his real name and I know roughly where he lives , I see him often in Shrewsbury walking around aimlessly , I remember back in the early nineties him sleeping rough and me asking him if all was ok , he just nodded and looked down again , my heart went out to him in later life but what could I say or do at that time ?.

It was going around a few of us what was happening , tony was now Simons mate as I was going around with Brian , Clive , Aidy and Martin after school , doing the same old tricks of stealing bikes and food from Safeways while tony kept his nose clean .

His Dad was on the brink of disowning him as he just married a new woman; tony was deciding which name to keep Simcoe or Dodd

Dec 1980.

Went with tony to the swimming baths on permission from Besford.

On the way back we stole a triumph stag from the swimming pools car park , tony opened it with a key we called an FS key , why I do not know but I used the same FS key to steal Mini's , Avengers , Moggy minors and anything really predating 1978 .

We took the Stag (tony driving) to Telford doing 120ish up the old A5 which in most parts is a straight road ,I was literally shitting myself when tony thought it was hilarious, (I'm sure he had a death wish)both of us little enough not to able to see over a very squat car ,our asses literally touching the floor in the car , I'm sure tony had to place his swimming towel under his ass to see , I just looked (if you could see me that is)gormless .

We ended up in Stafford railway station car park late at night but before the pubs closed , bored by then and probably thinking what are we going to tell them at Besford , bugger it all , so we robbed the train station newsagents of mars bars , and whatever we could lay our hands on , we didn't smoke then so left the park drives and embassy regals behind and headed back to Shrewsbury , we actually managed to get back without getting caught , amazing , Don't hold your breath .

We parked the car around the corner from Besford and used it a few times thereafter, tony teaching me how to drive properly down the old potts way scrap yard and laundry lane where we mainly hid out.

Laundry lane had a abandoned building next to the old salop laundry, we made fires, stole food to cook on it and this is where the stag bought it, Tony just had enough of it saying we would get caught one day as it was looking like 2 weeks since we stole it, so the idiot torched it when I was gathering wood for the fire.

We didn't need the fire as the car went up like guy faulks thoughts.

We ran and ran as fast as we could over the little reabrook bridge towards Besford, not wanting to get caught on this one as a desirable car and the book would have been thrown at us.

The next night it was a targa roof fiat X19 , D plate registrated , we had a walk around and managed to find this on a drive in meole brace , oh wow the keys in it , we pushed it out of the drive and away we went , this time heading to Chester and made it all the way , no bypass then it was the A5 basically up to chirk through Whittington then back roads to

Chester as I think the main bypass was being built around Wrexham then , we had trouble navigating around that area .

But I do know this adventure very very well; this would stick in any ones head.

When tony was driving I placed my hands under the passenger seat and low and behold I really could not believe what I found (I felt it first and instantly knew what it was) , the shock of bringing up a bank money sack full of 50p pieces , we stopped in a quite lane and counted , a total of approx £280-ish , we were rich , the country was ours , we would never ever return to Besford house ever again , freeeee , we could even afford to smoke now .

We ended up on our first leg in Chester the following day after sleeping in the car near chirk 2 x 12-14 Yr olds living it up in a sports car, better than the stag as we could see out of the windows in this car, it was purposefully made by fiat for us two, just us two, no one else just us two.

Chester was fun , we spent most of the cash in an amusement arcade and lost most of our cash in the amusement arcade , gutted (them penny falls still sucker me in to this day), but no worries as we still had plenty of money to explore the country.

We took the roof off and carried on our jolly way heading towards Liverpool, we went in one of the Mersey tunnels, started to get worried in here as we thought it was a road you had to pay to go through, all the signs saying have money ready.

Oh shit , we came to a queue and saw that a man was taking money from the cars , tony talking to me constantly to calm down and not to panic , I handed him 50p , we rolled up to the booth casually paid the fee of 5p I think , the booth man did not bat an eye lid but who did bat an eye lid was the copper looking straight at me on the left of me standing in front of a 4x4 police land rover car which had Tunnel written all over it .

The eye contact was just too long; I witnessed the copper getting in the car, oh poo.

Panicking again, the uncontrollable shaking.

Tony was also slightly panicking when I told him but luckily for us the copper went down the tunnel so we decided that it would be best if we didn't go to Liverpool, so we turned back to Chester but took the longer route through the other tunnel or we may have made a mistake, drove around a bit and went back through the same tunnel, I forget

I don't forget me driving for a few miles and parking up by the sea near Holywell somewhere, shopping spree again.

This time we went into a sports shop and brought loads of Shrewsbury town football club merchandise, (why you ask, well don't ask – I detested football at that time).

We attempted to get lager but ended up arguing with the shop owner, tony waving the stolen car keys at him saying he was old enough but to no avail.

But we still had bags full of the stuff (money), we spent the day by the beach, it was a school day so again looked upon by our elders, we decided that was too much so headed back to the car.

The roof was still down so like the dukes of hazard we leaped over the doors to get in , full of so much confidence that we would make it to our next destination which we decided south Wales , we made so many plans

From know where an army of police arrived in the car park , a BMW police car pulled up to block us in from behind , 2 burly coppers on the left , 2 burly coppers on the right grabbing through the open roof , games up .

They were extremely shocked to see 2 little round faced juveniles sitting at the wheel; I remember the shock on their faces so well.

Another lecture, another court date to follow, which we had to go up to Chester for, then they transferred it to Shrewsbury juvenile court, that would come after Christmas in Feb. 1981.

Dec 1980 (looking at my files it was a busy month for me).

Quote Mr Pugh Dec 15th 1980. For social enquiry report for court

Staff at Besford house have expressed concern that timothy has not become close with any member of staff , despite efforts to achieve this it is possible that frequent weekends at home has meant that timothy has little investment at Besford house and recently his weekends have been reduced to try to alter this situation .

There have been concerns over Timothy's behaviour and his offending in particular and attempts have been made to try to understand the reasons for this behaviour.

Since the offences for which he appears today timothy has absconded again with 2 boys from Shrewsbury and is being questioned by the police in relation to car theft , it would seem from his recent behaviour that timothy needs more and closer supervision , it is there for proposed that timothy be admitted into the Vineyard observation and assessment unit in wellington , Telford , for a period of assessment , with a view to a more appropriate future placement , this is being proposed at the moment .

Mr A was happy about this and lewdly told me very often that it would be ok and it would be nice to cuddle before I left either back home or to Telford, I quite remember the last few weeks knowing this man, I witnessed another assault on a friend of mine in the month of December 1980.

Mr A asked me and a few others to tidy up the back area of the house, kitchen area and clean the side driveway and the field and sheds would be done the following day.

I remember this point in my life as it would change (at the time better for me for the near future)

We tended not to do as we were told but made it look like we were doing something

(Busy boys doing nothing) if we looked too keen the staff would have us out every day cleaning leaves up and painting etc.

A friend decided he wanted a ciggie and the only safe place for this was at the back of the Shed in the evergreen bushes as that's where everyone went to smoke, we took the longest route following the brick wall so we didn't get seen by anyone on the field or from the side windows of the house, I remember only 1 spot in the bottom corner that you had to run for 10yrds under the naked trees as all others were either holly bushes or hawthorn.

We went to the back of the shed whilst my friend lit up his bit of a ciggie , where he got that dimp from I do not know but it was enough for a couple of drags for him and one for me , it was disgusting .

It was not a surprise to hear the noise from inside the shed as we where directly at the back , it was a corrugated tin at the rear unlike the rest of the building being wood , it was gone in places due to rot or rusted out screws so we had a peep to see Mr A going down on a very good friend who I went to school with , Aidy broke out in laughter while my eye was at the gap in the tin and Mr A and my old friend looked directly at me , I'm sure he could tell it was me but it was Aidies laughter which bellowed out .

We ran , forgetting the bushes , we went straight over the grass to the back of the house laughing a lot then picked up our brooms and shovel , Mr A came bounding around the corner and grabbed me and Aidy by the arms and marched and dragged us to the shed .

I often wonder if any other members of staff witnessed this but I very much doubt it as I think only 2-3 staff in any one time.

He slammed the door behind him and clouted Aidy around the head , hard really hard , so naturally I started to back away to the bottom corner of the shed , Aidy was crying uncontrollably on the floor saying he would not say anything to anyone , I remember Mr A was screaming at me about it's about time I got what my school friend was doing and getting , he started to raise his hand at me but thank heavens that Aidy got up , did a bunk and slammed the door behind him which stopped him beating me again , but he just kept coming at me , grabbed me around the throat , screeching at me that I will be getting the same before I leave , he started to rub me up asking if I liked it , I really do not what else I was thinking apart from it was not me who laughed outside , why me again .

I don't remember what happened next either Aidy came back with staff or he was disturbed about Aidy running out but I do have reports of my absconding in the few days.

And why you ask is that a good thing that happened in my life?

We got whilst at school at some time a contact to take cars we had stolen to a bloke and he would give us cash , this seemed to good to be true but gullible as we were we had to give it a go .

This was the ideal time to try this out as I was eager to run away after being threatened.

I and Brian a night or two after the threat from Mr A just happened upon a ford sierra, it was modern and new-ish looking, that is when we thought we would try out the dealer.

We only had an address and it was 2am in the morning but it was best to drive at night than in the morning so we made our way to the garage, it was around 40 miles away on the A5.

I'm not going to tell you which way from Shrewsbury as this man (or son) still has the garage, same signs, and same sort of cars, really weird to see him 35 years later still going.

We stayed at the garage until they opened up at 8am and then the knob of a garage hand said we had to get the car to a field 3 miles up the road to meet his boss, this was a bit nerve racking as it was rush hour around the garage and roads looking pretty full , Brian also having to sit on some sort of cushion to see , the garage had some young lad who was thick as shit as we must have pulled into 2-3 off main road drive ways but we did as we were told and drove the car to a farmer's field to be told by the garage hand that he lived in the house next to the farmer – Eh.

We waited for the bloke to arrive, he looked over the car, we had the keys to this car, where we got the car from I do not know but we got it anyway.

He offered us £50, Brian said no, it would be pointless to bringing out more for that as it would cost us to get back, he then said £100, oh yes we said yes to that.

That started a very long relationship; it got me out of many scrapes in the future whilst at the mount and St Gilberts.

I will probably tell you later but I made thousands from this man and we got quite acquainted over 6 years.

Who can I turn to and where can I stay?

I heard a place is open all night and all day

There's a place you can go where the cops don't know.

You can act really wild; they don't treat you like a child

Runaway Boys (Credit, stray cats Dec 1980, I remember everyone used to sing this to me)

I have just done my research and it was in the charts Christmas 1980, wow my memory for records is amazing.

My Time was limited at Besford after Mr A's antics and I did not stay to much at the place knowing that one day I would either have to succumb to the house masters needs or just carry on running away, I tried whistle blowing about the housemasters but to no avail, I was constantly running away to the weir or the air raid shelter, friends helping out as much as possible.

School time was very limited, hence the bad reports from Mr Revell.

The final straw was a week or two before I was sent to the vineyards Mr A came into my room saying that I would be leaving soon and he would like to make me happy before I leave, I explained to him he was not the first one here that has tried it on with me and I had loads of brothers who would sort him out, he didn't try again, he left, the dirty pervert left my room, I was shocked.

I saw him again in early 2000-ish whilst travelling up to Shrewsbury from London for a weekend with the family I stopped at the services on the M54, he was sitting with 2 other men in the cafe area (totally different now I see), we looked directly at each other, his eyes went passed mine but I could not stop staring at him, knowing this was the same bloke who tried it on with me on quite a few occasions.

I felt like going up and saying something to embarrass him in front of his mates but I also thought he may be a doppelganger as it was now 15-17 years later, at the time I felt like following him, getting his address and searching him out, mainly to see if he had young kids at the house like grandchildren etc, (I had 3 myself by then) but then maybe beating the fuck out of him when he's alone.

The following day at Besford (10/12/80 , and one of my last days at Besford) we (I cannot name this person)decided to do one more heist on the Granada bingo hall , we knew we could get quite a bit of money from here , a friend's mother worked there so we quizzed him over time about the set up .

I absconded (as usual) from Besford to a pre-arranged meeting with a friend at 10pm, this is when the bingo hall closed and we could wait in wappy Philips yard (that was like a junk shop taking over an acre of land by the river opposite the bingo hall, a very dangerous building to be in, very rickety as it seemed to be precaresly hanging over the river, inside was a warren of rooms smelling of rat piss.

Most of it built from corrugated sheets and old pieces of timber. (As pic)

It was fun for us as it had giant advertising boards at the front on Smithfield road overlooking the bingo hall , we could see out but they could not see in due to the type of panels wappy had placed in between the advertising hoarding

It sold everything from wellies , comics ,rat piss , Barbour jackets ,rat shit ,wind chimes ,weal's disease, salt loads and loads of road salt , clothes of allsorts all smelling of damp oh and rat piss , everything was just thrown wherever , even wappy didn't know what he had ,

Apart from Midda in the market this place was just the best , I forget the amount of times I went in here without taking anything , it was more like a giant den, I liked that man so much , I think we got on great , himself and Dave merryfield who owned the boxing club/arcade , cafe next to the castle , we used to use it like a social club as none of the housemasters knew about it , Dave was very accommodating as he knew my father well .

Unbeknown to him we used to use the electronic lighter clickers on the 2p & 10p fruit machines to clock up credits , he did find out a couple of times but we played more than we put in . I do not think we even left with money as it then got shovelled back into the new space invaders table top machines he had or we just got bored .

So back to the bingo hall, we scaled the drain pipe at the back of the hall and managed to force a window open, knowing this went into the staff toilet.

Now this place is massive, corridors running around the old cinema house (Beatles once played here I hear), we ended up in the bingo hall itself after scrambling around in the dark corridors, the large bingo room was lit up a bit so we started at the bar filling up boxes of liquor then went opposite to the canteen area and filled up more boxes of chocolate, crisps and raiding the float in the till (£16.40 on the charge sheet).

We managed also to turn every light on in the main hall and corridors, knowing no one outside could see the lights on.

The foyer by the front door was in darkness but it did not stop up breaking into the £100 fruit machines which were partly hidden to the front treble doors, we filled a box from the cash out area full of coins and placed this by the emergency back door, we were so stealth about everything, we had all night to do this.

The amount of times people walked past the main doors casually looking to the left or right and not seeing what was going on just feet from them .

We knew roughly where the office was, we knew also that the door leading to the office was alarmed, mmm I remembering arguing with my accomplice about how we go about doing this, so.

We went to the adjoining toilet , went up through the ceiling polystyrene tiles , crawled along the roof area and took the ceiling tiles away from above the office , and down we jumped onto the managers table in the main office , BINGOOOOOO , we found the safe in the cupboard , 5ft tall , so we managed to drag it out of the cupboard area ,looked around it and thought " now how do you open a safe if you have no key" , we put the managers chair on the table clambered up through the gap and went back to the main hall , that was a waste of time .

We collected everything from the bar and canteen and placed these by the back door , it was looking like a very good booty , by this time it was around 1am , the pubs across the way were now empty so we felt confident that hardly anyone would see us leaving out the back .

Stupidly we decided to have a look up stairs at the back (the old cinema projection room) as we were playing around with a 50s projector we heard the dreaded "we know you are in here as we have your items with us "oh shit.

We ran as fast as we could to the back of the bingo hall along the hidden corridor , ending up again by the staff toilets , out of the window and down the pipe , which happened to be higher than then we went in ? .

I made it to the bottom, my friend did not even make it out, I was collared by the back gate, nearly very nearly escaped, police station then back to Besford it was.

(Besford Report., Timothy came back to Besford in the company of a police officer at 3am in a dirty muddy state.)

He was an aggressive towards us when questioned about the £16.40 in his pocket saying he earnt it at his grandmothers the previous day....

We later found out that they had put a pressure alarm carpet in the Granada bingo office, as soon as you stood on it the silent alarm would go off.

I was not flavour of the month with my friend's mother; luckily we would not see each other for quite some time.

Dec 15th 1980. (Goodbye Belvidere school, hello freedom?)

I got admitted to the vineyards for 5 weeks to be assessed, I didn't mind this place as my brother went here to be assessed and him telling me that it was ok to be here and lots of girls would be present, so here started my 5 week stint at a place I would say a very nice place to be.

I do not remember to much about running away from the vineyards , but files and reports do not have to many dates on them either so this section may be mixed up a bit , I will try to place in order as I remember it .

Report No 1 (15/12/1980)

Timothy has settled well in his 24 hours he has conversed freely with staff.

There are only a small number of children upon his admission so very easy to get to know the ones he does not know he seems happy and relaxed.

He washes without being told

18/12/1980 (I must have just gone in for the day then I went back in on the 18th?)

I was 5ft 4", weighed 7st, 6Lbs, so I was a strapping lad at 14.

Home life according to reports was not good , family in debt , Brothers not working , support from social services had stopped , my parents relationship was really bad , mother going through another divorce from the same man (my father) many separations and many reconciliations .

I was apparently in awe of my brothers even though they used to beat me, my father was still not a part of my life, and he mainly lived in Holland now.

I was closer to my sister than my brothers when I did go home for the weekend, I mainly stayed at my grandmothers as she over indulged me , mother often stayed at grandmothers but she abused the privilege according to my reports so my grandmother disowned her for a while , probably because at the time she was going out with a bloke who abused her physically , my brothers sorted this problem out by beating him up , he left shortly afterwards , my mother told me a few years ago that he had died so she must have been keeping a track of him , even after 30 years.

My Mother had a fantastic memory, she could remember aunties and uncles from the 50s/60s, all the people she grew up with and neighbours to the many houses she lived in and frequented, she refrained from telling me my very early life saying she could not remember.

Report The Vineyards, 22nd/23rd Dec 1980 (I have combined reports from both vineyards and social services.

22/12/80. (1 week staying the vineyards.)

Vineyards , Timothy has settled in well enjoying the intimacy we have , we have 5 children in at the moment , visit by Mr Pugh , Timothy's social worker who spent some time with him and mentioned how well behaved he is .

Tim has brought a few things like his record player and records which he is now bored of so loans out to other children , he keeps himself to himself , he is clean ,seems intelligent , has a very good sense of humour .

He is occasionally enuretic a fact he first tried to hide but quickly got over his embarrassment , he has no problems getting up in the morning as he goes to bed very late after reading his comics , he usually lies on his stomach with his hands beneath him , he does not snore , he cleans his bed area in the morning , he eats well but never seems to have second helpings .

He treats the cottage and others people's property with respect, He needs to clean his teeth more often.

The daily chores he has to do he begrudges but does do them, he is good on time keeping, he is always in the place he should be.

In summery timothy has kept well within the bounds of acceptable behaviour and therefore not been a problem at all on the other hand.

He has not given anything of himself during his short stay with us , he is just going through the motions of daily living and one wonders whether he is just behaving and possibly there is more to Tim then he is allowing us to see .

First report

My meeting was with about 8-10 adults, oh wait a mo I will find the file and count them.

Mr Addison, Principal social worker officer

Mr Malcolm, Team leader for O & A

Mr Carran, Head teacher 0 & a school

Mr Cotterall, Principal, Besford House

Mr Pugh, social worker.

Mr Adams, Houseparent 0 & A.

Mr Revell, Belvidere Headmaster.

Miss Curl, Educational Psychologist.

I don't recall this meeting but basically in other reports miss curl and Mr Revell were saying I was immature but the conclusion was.

Timothy is a boy of average intellectual ability with a reasonable level of attainments, he presents himself as a quite lively and imaginative boy but this seems to ease when in the company of others older than him.

The conference concluded that Timothy should reside at the Mount school after further assessment.

That same day the police called around with a charge sheet, (I'm so glad they came after the meeting), mother writes in a note to the vineyards she gave to the police when they went knocking at my mother's door first as they (the police) did not know where I was (weird after so many times taking me back to Besford house.

"Can you address the below letter to Timothy Draycott please".

I have heard that Timothy will not be allowed to come to my house for Christmas , would it be possible for him to stay at his grans the police officer says he will wait for an answer and bring it back to me , sincerely , Sue Draycott.

23rd Dec 1980

You are charged jointly with Tony Simcoe (ne;Dodd) enter a property in Trench in Telford on 14/11/1980 namely belonging to Mr and Mrs Simcoe and steal £15.20 , a pair of sunglasses , a cigarette case and food to the value of £10 belonging to Mrs Simcoe .

Date and time of burglary 14th November 1980, date of court hearing 23rd January 1981.

I spent Christmas 1980 at the vineyards with a few others who were either orphaned or could not go home due to family problems like myself, I liked the vineyards, it was peaceful, no staff trying it on with me so basically no abusers, no shouty staff, all was calm here, I did however go to my grandmothers for new years eve.

05/01/1981

A day out for myself and a social worker to the Mount to see what I thought of it, I can't remember this but report says that I seemed happy but also unsure about the place.

I got naggy and irritable when they said I could be here as soon as the end of the month.

Even though I detested the head master I was concerned that I would lose my place at Belvidere school, not really wanting to go back to Besford house I really wanted to stay at the vineyards but that was only an assessment centre, my grans was the next option but social reports state I would reoffend if left to my own devices.

07/01/1981. (See what I mean about the writing, this is what I have to try to decipher)

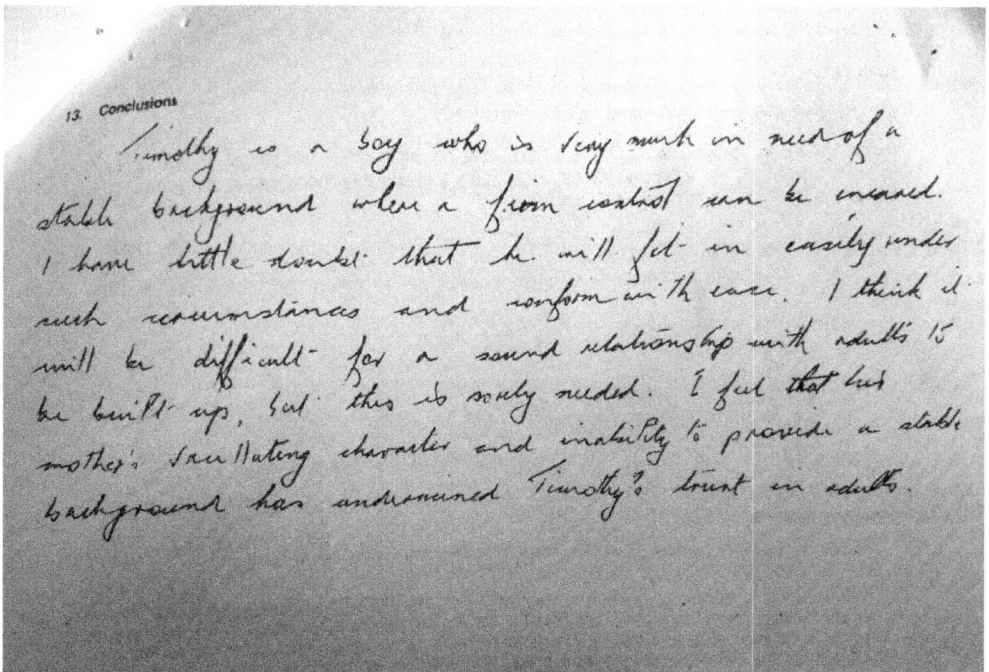

13. Conclusions

 Mr Revells conclusion report to the vineyards 07/01/1981, let me know if it says anything bad, I can see the word timothy twice and difficult for a sound relationship with a? To be built up, oh blah blah blah Revell, he goes on to say.

That I was only interested in toys and playing army games , not interested in anything requiring patience or concentration because of an inconsistent nature .

His lackadaisical approach and come-day, go-day attitude make marked progress difficult.

He is gregarious with other children, polite, friendly, open and ingenuous.

Outward going scared of brothers, happy go-lucky always cheerful overtly so in that it is probably an unreality world into which he enters.

He has never had to face the consequences of his actions as long as he can maintain this facade , from first entering the school there were instances of persistent and premeditated pilfering from within and out of the school , fairly easily detected once known , over the last twelve months instances within the school have decreased .

Well I must say that was not nice in places and you have hit a nerve here, I'm sure like other times I thought I was a model pupil? , but to say that I like playing army games, no way.

I pretended to be either six million dollar man , Bodie from the professionals(I suppose he is army being in Ci5) or bungle from rainbow (I do a great impression) , I hated the army .

16/01/1981.

I was sat in a room on my own for a couple of hours 10.45am-2.15pm to undertake a Burt test, Neale analyses, Vernon's maths test, and something called a Schonell spelling test.

Well what a shock to see my results and to get high in accuracy, rate and comprehension, better than average they said.

My mother attended that day with a few others to talk about me in depth.

I have reports from social services and from the vineyards , but they all wrote like Drs at the time , very hard to decipher my reports , just waffling on about me not going back to Shrewsbury and I will end up at the mount , either before D.C or after .

So blank life until 16/02/81 and then the social services blank my paperwork out in abundance so I do not what went on there , I totally understand them blanking others names but most of my vineyards reports have been blanked.

I have a court appearance to deal with on the 20/03/81

These being at juvenile court

 Burglary – guilty, theft – guilty, burglary of a dwelling, theft of a cycle

for these I got a 1 year conditional discharge and costs of £4.00 but 2 sentences where differed from earlier court dates from the 12/12/80, oh dear I'm going to get sentenced with them as well and I did, with another care order, just another care order in my eyes, what's the point in having another when you already have one?.

The Vineyards went by very quick, I did not abscond or do anything really troublesome at the home (I did when I went home for New Year though).

Another 5 weeks of my life I knew little about went by , a not so memorable time really at that place , I could gap fill that part of my life here and tell you about my dad's jack Russell Gus but that's just about a jack Russell called Gus , please read on .

I had to go to the 1990s built housing estate which now stands on the old vineyards site (opposite Morrison's supermarket, Wellington) to see if I could get memories but to no avail, I just sat near the houses looking blankly at them, on one occasion thinking about a poem I now know to be a Pam Ayres poem over and over in my head? , I jotted it down whilst I was sitting there thinking where the hell did that come from.

The tiger stalks through the night

Delivers a hideous bite.

And there on his paws.

Are hideous claws

But apart from that, he's alright

knowing the layout of each building , now knocked down , I remember arriving and leaving into the main house and reading comics in the house by the main road but very little else .

It was all about keeping an eye on you for 6 weeks, basically a total waste of money.

If I find more reports regarding what I did at the vineyards I will enter them, they all seem to be either missing from my life or the ones I have blanked off.

Court date 20/03/81

OBSERVATIONS. (From Vineyard social worker)

Timothy presents himself in a confident way the only outstanding feature is that he does not concern himself about his future.

His approach to work was almost wholly acquiescent , he did not question anything placed before him , he tackled all with a high level of motivation , he did however leave the impression always that the level of concentration which he brought to these subject area's was fairly superficial .

He is a very competent reader and excels in that area , he would not find it difficult to adjust in a comprehensive school , nevertheless his ability in written work is very low , and is on par with very bad spelling , he has a poor style of writing often mixing up CurSive and priNt style writing , his writing is very immature .

Timothy's drawing is well above his age bracket and I feel he will go far in Art.

(I did, I got an A level in art).

He has recently taken a motorcycle session (I don't remember that*), cancelling his swimming lessons and indoor games which involved co-operation with other children.*

Tim has kept well within the bounds of acceptable behaviour, he has no management problems he hardly puts a foot wrong (TD - I'm sure that will change soon).

He is a great conversationalist, he will answer non searching questions but will not talk in length nor will he go into any great depth , he is a willing worker he will carry out his job if he cannot find an excuse to get out of it , and then he does not do a good job.

As he grows in confidence he is beginning to join in and enjoy physical banter but on a very minimal level, he gets embarrassed when you praise him and often fidgets with his hands in his pockets.

Tim refuses to talk to staff about his family and friend life in Shrewsbury , he goes home for weekends , he went home for the new year and no reported troubles or problems , the telephone conversations timothy had before Christmas to his family were long but we notice Tim has made no phone calls in the past week , when questioned about this he walks away without saying anything .

He has now began to watch television and ignoring tasks put out for him , he will watch hours if you let him , or he will read books or comics , Timothy has been very quite in this week after the new year .

His relation to teaching staff has been normal , his attitude towards other children in the unit have been bland , he has chosen to work on his own in spite of the fact he was given lots of opportunities to get involved in group activities.

In our conclusion it is difficult to assess timothy in his short time here with the behaviours he has shown in Besford House and secondary school as well as a social environment.

He presents here as a likable youth, very clever at times but in times of depression and after visits home he becomes solitude and will not interact with anyone.

He is either unwilling or unable to make a very substantial investment in relationships.

Chapter whatever, IVE LOST COUNT

Up to the 21st Jan 1981 – Movement to the mount boys home & Manor house school

I am not looking forward to writing this section and have been dreading it since started to write my memoirs so I have come to pathos, (20/09/2019) Cyprus to get peace and tranquillity in my thoughts, along with 1200 pages of historical reports and a great excuse to get some sun and Cypriot wine which I hear is very nice this time of year, get more sun and think of my passed girlfriend Amanda and my gorgeous mother.

During my visit I may enter a few items totally off subject , sorry if this breaks up the book a bit but I can hardly resist making the reader a touch jealous of me sunning it up.

But just arrived 6 hours ago (its 7am now) I notice they drive on the left , the plug sockets are the same , large old people swim in the sea at the crack of dawn wearing Speedos , they eat cake for breakfast and smoke horrendous smelling cigarettes in the cafe bars .

Right let's get back to it , after another coffee me thinks (they serve coffee with iced water (I don't understand that , how am I supposed to get wired)and not after I have mentioned some brat bloke opposite me swigging down the local Keo lager beer , he's on his fourth (at 7am) weirdo , I have a golden rule never to drink before midday .

If you are easily offended I would skip this whole section and a few chapters , I apologise about the probable bad language and graphic detail , I feel if I do not give an accurate account the book would be incomplete and as mentioned I am very truthful in my book so I cannot miss anything I remember .

Mr M Walters – Educational psychologist addressed to the Mount Boys School.

*"You will shortly receive the Q & A on the above named boy who previously lived in the Shrewsbury area and attended for a short time Belvidere school , we have approached Charlton and Orleton park school who cannot except timothy , Mr Thornton has kindly agreed to accept him on roll immediately , there may be some problems fitting in on some groups, They are most grateful to Mr Thornton and his staff in advance for the help offered with regard to placement of Timothy and hope he will respond by performing well in his new school . ...***Oh Boy did I respond.**

(Going forward slightly but relevant to this section) Social workers report 29th April 1981.

There have been no significant changes in timothy's family's material circumstances , however during the past 2 months of Timothy's admission into the mount there has been considerable disruption not only from Timothy's constant absconding but his fighting at school and sneaking back to Besford house to pick up Brain to take him out for joyrides ,

Besford can do nothing about this apart from phone the police if timothy arrives as they know he would be an absconder.

Mrs Draycott is understandably quite harassed and anxious at present and is rapidly being exhausted by her son's behaviour.

She accepts timothy needs to be moved to avoid certain detention centre sentences he would receive for any further misdemeanours.

Night 1 at the mount boys home , (21/01/81) wellington , this being my first ever night at the Mount , they seemed to think (according to Mr. Pugh , one of many key workers/social workers or general hippies who didn't know what to do with me , it was a more structured regime specifically for male adolescents they say in a report (have a read , it's interesting - scanned below) .

- 3 -

SUBJECT:

Timothy presents as a friendly and pleasant boy. He was assessed by the County Psychologist following persistent lying and stealing at Infant School. On 1st June, 1979, Timothy appeared before Shrewsbury Juvenile Court and was made the subject of a Supervision Order. His commitment to supervision was initially disappointing but latterly showed some improvement. A further Supervision Order with provisions for Intermediate Treatment was made on 11th January, 1980.

Timothy was then involved in a three month programme from February to April which involved ten after-school sessions and one weekend away. The aim was to supervise the children through involvement in activities with them. It was apparent that he enjoys and is capable of, constructive activity and is amenable to positive influences in a structured setting.

Following the imposition of the Care Order on 27th June, 1980, Timothy appeared unconcerned about going away from home, at the time he felt he could respond to help by changing his behaviour in a different environment. However, the placement at Besford House has been a failure with numerous abscondings and the committal of further misdemeanours. On 15th December, 1980, Timothy was transferred to the Vineyard Observation and Assessment Centre in Telford, for a period of assessment; a more appropriate placement. On 21st January, 1981, Timothy was transferred to The Mount Community Home, Wellington, where there is a more structured regime, specifically for male adolescents. It is hoped that the positive response to the more structured environment of the Vineyard will be continued at The Mount. The removal of Timothy from his home town and the company of his usual companions will help to reduce the opportunities for them to stimulate each other into wrongdoing. Consequently, the distance from home will strengthen the rewards for positive behaviour such as weekend leave.

CONCLUSION:

Despite the impression given by his pleasant manner and ability to converse with adults. Timothy is a boy with little self control. The lack of consistency in his upbringing the disruptions of home life have contributed largely to his unsatisfactory behaviour. However, he has shown the capability to respond favourably to structured situations where expectations of him are clearly delineated and since his scholastic performance is adequate, it is felt that he would benefit from the opportunity to progress at the Mount Community Home.

Signed .....

In the rugby club "oh yeah lovely I thought, no different to the last place.

I hated rugby then and I ended up playing squash in tournaments and basketball for our local village then town, then down to see the Harlem globetrotters at Wembley arena, but I will mention this much later at chapter 2.

But at that time I just wanted a garden area so I could be alone in my own world, a keen gardener from my granddad Harold and Wilf with his bloody geraniums for the flower show, I hate them flowers.

He (Mr)took me around the place , all the other kids starring at me , I know what they were thinking as I thought the same later whenever someone new arrived ." another lamb to the slaughter , maybe I didn't think that at the time but it was as near as dammit .

The first thing before unpacking was to shower in the open plan shower at the back of the Mount house.

It was like a lean to attached to the back of the house , back wall full of windows , opposite a straight 15ft tiled wall , old iron wall hangers on the wall , I'm sure - out of reach

(Social services who took over the building back in 2002 refused me taking photos of the building, hatches, hallways etc after I told them I was a resident in the early 80s, I had to apply for permission – which I didn't at the time as that is when I applied for the files I am reading from, and roughly the same time accusations were going around about various Children's homes in Shropshire), they got frightened I think as they were very panicky.

If remembering entering the mount I always think of Hitchcock's famous shower scene in the bates hotel , the tiles were like what you would get in a 1970s public toilet block , grubby ,stained grout and very open but these showers had no curtains ,(if they did I would Have run away more , go on play the Hitchcock shower scene music in your head now E , E , E , E , , go on now do the stabbing motion E, E , E , E) as I arrived so late in the day I was alone in the shower while I listened to the hustle and bustle of the mount children .

Mr D (you know what's coming when I only mention the initial don't you ?) , one of the housemasters at the time who interned and interviewed me after Mr Stokes , gave me fresh underwear , toiletries , towel etc before showing me my room and around the place again , telling me the out of bounds area (somewhere I eventually got to go to – oooh lucky me).

After dumping my kit on my bed he told me to strip from the clothes I had on and put fresh on , I did not have a lot as a majority of my things are still at the vineyards , they were due to be picked up today for me .

I stripped (as it's not unusual due to the amount of housemasters who have seen me in the buff) he took me to the shower told me to wash everywhere as it's a clean house compared to the others I had been to , and Ms (Stokes) likes all boys clean .

Here we go again more fuckin pervs to deal with; I've got to get out.

Mrs stokes reminded me of the mother to tom in tom and jerry cartoons where you only see her legs under a spinsters skirt – thomaaaaaaaaaasssse were yo at , you chasin mouse again , (We had to call Mrs Stokes , Ms).

She was bottom fat, varicose vein legs, slippers and fluffy socks, a skirt you would expect to find as a summer table cloth at Wimbledon.

In my view this house was the dirtiest (I'm not talking about the pervy staff , its gets worse but the actual home itself , dank and damp smelling)

Oh dear going off story again then I think.

Mr D insisted on staying in the shower room leaning against the window making sure I washed everywhere and when I say that I meant it , not only this time but on quite a few occasions came over to the lads and started to wash us , now luckily I had seen this thing going on , sometimes I thought it was natural as I have grown up with it , but I always said no to him washing me , once being quite forceful and being berated for it but my memory slips on this occasion as why I said no when others were saying yes .

I remember slightly an altercation in the shower and I ended up on the floor , but I know no details why I got myself on the floor or the argument I had with Mr D , I also said no to the house mistresses lifting up my shclong (that's a great word from my memories of a Mel brooks film I think) with a whipping stick as we got into the shower , we had to be inspected under our gonads before we went into the shower , yes you read correctly , before we went in the shower.

We queued up for a shower in a line after school along a 15ft bare corridor , 3 windows at the back running along that corridor , on hard cold tiles waiting for one of the 4 showers to be free , we had to hang our towels around 10ft before the shower leaving us naked waiting for a shower to be free , every boy got inspected under his nuts and then came a little light smack on the bum with the whip as we went in , this was not hard , more of a coaxing to get into the shower , so I can happily say that I do not think that was abuse , this was either done by the so called care ladies (dinner ladies or house mistress ,I'm sure they were the dinner or laundry ladies) " Come on boys clean under there also " was what I heard nearly every day for a few months

Or the dreaded Mr C, who unlike Mr A and B seemed to be at the Mount every time I was present. (Which was not a lot due the constant absconding?)

He was also a chunky bloke going on obese, (if today's BMI is anything to go by) balding hair, round face, always wore a black t-shirt, looking back on it year after year I think, knob.

I actually think he had a bed sit flat at the Mount home, but I could be wrong as I think a few key workers stayed overnight, maybe it was shift? Maybe I should look into the shift patterns but that's tedious as it would require me to apply to the council and further afield so I will carry on what I know.

There was one other house master that I cannot describe in any way as he is so describable so we will call him Mr D , as it sort of goes in order of the housemasters/mistresses/abusers.

(Let's see if I can get to the end of the alphabet?).

This bloke committed the most anuses of child abuse crimes I care to imagine.

We had fire hatches throughout the building; my room was top 3rd floor, left side as you are looking at the building.

This room had 3 single beds in an L shape room.

My bed was to the left of the fire door as you come through the fire door,_____(soon to be friend) was on the other side of the fire door.

These doors where approx 1.5mx1.5m so you had to virtually crawl through.

I was still quite fat and chunky but I remember going through them on a few occasions to visit late at night the rooms next door.

I could not walk through the main bedroom door as the housemaster's door (leading to his living room) was right next door to our bedroom door.

On a few occasions I witnessed the perv key worker coming through the hatch/door and grabbing my roommates hand and taking him back through the hatch.

The memories of these visits still haunt me as the crying that followed was not nice, I cried many times and wet the bed many times during my days at the mount (also berated many times for wetting the bed, weirdly enough I usually wet the bed whilst being either shouted at on the night after lockdown or whilst being stared at by the evening key worker when he dragged a lad out for an hour or 2 – dependant who it was).

I was a very scared person at the time always thinking that maybe I would be next. it was a thought I thought about a lot at that time and shared it with many friends who lived in Shrewsbury , I was really concerned about the mount but hey ho , let us not reminiscence over them thoughts I am thinking currently , so let's carry on in the morning after a few Keo's this evening.

(Keo is a local beer 5.5% (what English people drink , Cypriot ,tastes like piss water , I need to find real craft ale) .

The sash windows at the Mount you could not lift up more than 5-7", meaning to me no escape, I am used to running away when I liked but this was different.

The shouting was like the future detention centre I would attend , (they got rid of Borstal the year before I went and changed them all to detention centres – later – probably chapter 211 , the shouting was constant if you did something wrong .

The evening supper was terrible for me then, kids getting told off for the most minor things but I look back on and think, maybe that was correct.

No elbows or forearms on tables (at all), no making of sandwiches at the table, you had to place the bread on the plate, the bacon on the bread and cut and eat, our cutlery had to placed in a certain way when starting, finishing and during our meal, obvious one, never speak with your mouth full so no one ever spoke as we had little time to wolf this gruel down.

We could not cut up our food until it was ready to place in our mouths, so no pre cutting, we must rest during our meal to drink a little, and we had to eat quite.

These rules I still mainly stick to 40 years later I don't know if this is a good thing or not as it does really bring back memories when I see what I am doing sometimes at restaurants, cafes and whatnot, no arms or elbows on tables, no making a sandwich from your plate, if having a burger this would be cut on the plate and my cutlery weirdly always goes to the place it is supposed to do.

When dining nowadays I always feel I am being constantly watched as we were in the Mount , I feel very uncomfortable when dining out but not at all when delivering foods to hundreds of people as with my catering company later in life .

(I don't advise writing on a beach with loads of paperwork surrounding you and the sun out glaring my laptop so I'm going to gather this up and go to a local cafe bar – nice).

Doors locked at around 5-6pm and throughout during tea/supper, if you wanted to do a runner (abscond) it had to be in the day or early evening.

22/01/81

SECOND day at the Mount. (RGP – Social report)

Telephone call from John Malcolm Timothy has gone AWOL on a school trip to Shrewsbury, the police have been informed.

The school trip in question was to Frankwell quays (not to the lovely chippy what used to be there but to the old stew building ,do look it up , it dates back to the 1400s and has brilliant history , it's amazing .

Me and tony have stolen a few cars from Frankwell as old mechanics garages used to vacate a load of areas where the theatre now stands, easy to get into the garages and keys usually left in the office on a pin board.

I happened to be next to the garages whilst on this school trip , I casually walked up to a car , got in it and stole it , I took a beat up little red mini , why I do not know as I got about a mile in it heading out of town , it was banging and clattering going up the hill of Frankwell island and I was attracting attention at midday , I was out of that car in a shot and started to run along the river , at least I got away , I probably stayed overnight in the Air raid shelter again .

23/01/81, HV, Social worker

Went to Mrs Draycott to see if Timothy had reappeared, she said she had persuaded him to go back and that he had gone back to the Mount.

I then called the Mount to timothy had returned, we then went to the vineyards to pick up the remainder of his belongings

Timothy tells me he really does not want to back to the mount and could he stay at the vineyards or his mothers who would be eager to have him back.

I explained that the care order was in place to help him and the now deferred court date for the 20th March with the extra charges would need to be addressed.

Timothy's anxiety seems to have arisen when talking about the Mount

The social services then decided to blank out and cover another 2 months of reports (I wonder what it says under that blanking off?)

Lad's parents came to see him one weekend; I broke into his parents car stole everything and hid the booty under my bed, opening it later in the night after we all got interrogated at the supper table, - contents – women's stuff.

I gave him the stuff back the next day and he promised not to tell, just to tell his mum someone found it by the main gate, so opening up another questioning as someone from the outside world could have broken in the car (the car park is adjacent to the main roads of wellington town).

If no one admitted it all weekend privileges would be taken away and we would not have any home leave or rec (reclamation time – on pool table, no TV etc).

So dumbass and nice as I was I admitted it.

The caning I got from Mr D that night was the worst, I think off my dad, I think of Mr Harper at the lancs, I think of Mr Revell at Belvidere and Mr C at St Gilberts when I think of the beatings I got but this was the reason I did not stay at the mount for very long, this is the reason I complained to the social services key worker at the time about what was going.

The night of my beating was when MR (stokes)` was out and after I admitted that I just opened the door and having a wise crack about the stealing but I never stole anything really as I returned it all – worthless crap , I was scared to admit the previous night at the dinner my actions .

When everyone was on Rec (recreation time)after my admission I was taken to see Mr D in MRs main office , as soon as the dinner lady had delivered me to his office after dinner (5-6pm) I was grabbed by the arm through the part opened door and thrown into the room , I cannot remember to much apart from him straggling me over the chest , shouting at me , ugly fat twat he was ,I know we thrashed around the room , banging into MRs table and ending up in the front window sill , sorry that's about it of my memories of that , I can presume but I can't , I'm not jcb row lings but I must have broke free in some way as I distinctly think of him pulling at me and hitting me on the arse with something whilst I'm trying to break free and grab at the door handle , I don't remember what followed but I do remember in a weird way .

(I'm sure it was this night that I ran away by forcing the kitchen windows that night of this abuse), Seeing him coming through the hatch late that night , ignoring me for my bed neighbour ,

I have questioned this in my head many many times over the past 40 odd years , why after the beating he did not pick on me that night after what we had just been through , me pretending to be asleep and him grabbing my bed neighbour , I so much wanted to do or say something on the night but looking back on it now , I was crying silently , turned away , it's a weird state that you freeze and let it carry on , so I think at the moment , this moment I will put it down to my age at the time and knowing the abusive goings on at my previous home , maybe it was the norm at the time , I haven't really gone into local abuse at homes in Shropshire whilst writing this as I did not want the thoughts of others , but as soon as I have written this I look more into the Besford house abuse highlighted in the Shropshire star at the time , which I found out about whilst working in London in 92-ish .

Social services have blanked off many pages from the 16/01/81 to 26/01/81

So I have to rely on crime reports to tell me my whereabouts, now where did I put them?

17/01/1981.

After talking to Timothy's friends in Castlefields, he was found to be hiding in an abandoned war time shelter next to the gay meadow, Shrewsbury town football club.

He looked well considering it was dark and damp , he was supplied by his friends with a sleeping bag , a gas camping stove , he seemed and was settled in ,Timothy has told us that his grandmother has been looking after him and he was only staying to get ready to go back to the mount . Cliff stokes would not take him in that night, Besford had agreed to have timothy for 1 night as long as he is picked him up ready for school the following day.

Cliff has mentioned that we should arrange a meeting regarding timothy being very problematic since his arrival...

Whaaat I'm looking into that, I'm sure I was the model pupil at the time? (T.D)

17/01/81 (yes the same night, I'm only staying for 1 night)

Apparently according to coinciding charge sheets with Social enquiry reports I have come to the conclusion that this WAS the night , I was in Besford for approximately 2 hours that night , I vaguely recall a friend saying that lainey had been looking for me (even though I had been gone for a quite awhile from Besford) , I ended up at martins (lainey) brothers house , I will mention myself and martins naughty antics throughout but at the moment I am sticking with what my reports state from police and social services .

Martins brother was berating him for going out with me at around midnight and I'm sure martin would have said he was taking me back to the boys home but I don't recall , I only recall the ford Cortina Mk5 (it was new so it must have been a Mk5)(sierras were my fav car to steal was not quite invented then) and lainey had the Vauxhall victor we stole that night , (dark blue for me , puke green and white for Laney) 1 being from the new housing estate next to the Shrewsbury police station , the other being from near belvidere school (1 mile from the police station), Ha you can't catch us . *(Famous last words)*

Being the tender age of around 14-ish I writ so many crimes of with the police, called at the time (and it may still be) T.I.C, taken into consideration.

They (police officers) say to you "Tim admit to this and we won't charge you for these other crimes "

Oh ok. (police writ off about 20-30 crimes that happened in town and I get charged with 1 , they are doing me a favour and I'm doing them a favour .)

o.m.g , I think the police had a field day every time I was brought in as I admitted to so much , I probably didn't do , but looking at my criminal record I probably did .

I will tell you what I remember of that night but I will rely on the reports to give the full account over a short space of time (7 days to be precise).

In our lovely easily stolen cars myself who by now was quite a masterful driver and martin managed to get to the church stretton hills , we lit a fire at the top of the longmynd , which is a fantastic beauty spot in Shropshire , long high hills and sheep shit in abundance.

Plenty of hiding places back then, now all the tracks are blocked off, but back then you could go off the beaten track and not be found (weirdly I have only courted 1 girl on the local beauty spot, Stretton hills and that was my beloved Amanda.)

We (me and Martin) ended up burning paperwork from martins car to get a fire going and kept us going for some time , and quite high (the fire being high , not us) , *(a few days later I would find out that we burnt the all of the files to a business owner who was moving offices , police and social workers really drilled me about doing this car theft , I shook my head many times on this , as I didn't steal the car , I didn't burn the paper and I didn't drive it to the edge of the hill , on that night I was at Besford all night ??*

I often think about that paperwork , as I think tax forms , business plans ,wage slips, etc etc from years and years , no computers back then , ouch , another juvenile crime massively regretted as I spent 16 years with my own business and I know the importance of paperwork.

Now considering we were 14 at the time , I was small and fat (but I'm sure I knew I was growing slowly) , and lainey being skinny and slightly taller than my short and fat , a farmer type bloke just shouted us from a short distance , we obliviously shat ourselves at the time but he shouted out that if we put the fire out and leave he will not phone the police , I think he was also shitting himself as he probably though we were thugs , but how did we not see his lights approaching ? , but we seen them leave, so hightailed we did and ended up what is now near the gliding club.

I remember me and lainey pushing his victor down the hill , the hill ended up being around a mile deep , we later found out the car was a right off , (obviously would be , stretton hills are high) , luckily no houses below , but we knew that ?.

The police took this crime into consideration a few weeks later, so basically I admitted it.

The Cortina I didn't want to part with , some cars you get attached to and do not want to burn , ring or throw off a quarry mountain edge but this was our spot to get rid of cars near the town (3 mile walk through fields and an old canal path , virtually direct to Besford) , so Haughmond quarry it had to be unless I was going to stay in hiding forever , the Mount was not a nice place to go back to and I don't think that was plaguing me at the time , it was the school , Hadley manor I really dreaded going back to , I knew as soon as I walked in the door I would probably end up fighting .

We set fire to the car as it was getting light, I got back to Besford, sneaked in, got picked up for school, met friends etc etc

I got grassed up to Mr stokes the following evening , I think to be liked and seem popular at the time , I told just to many kids at school about the previous nights activities , I had been given 2 many chances but did I ever listen , no , It came to bite me in the ass that night .

I think over the next few weeks the full arms of the law came down on me as my crime sheets seemed to think I was peeking at this given time in my life.

Social services records states numerous meetings at the Bates motel , (sorry I meant the Mount) ,in the short time I spent at the Mount my crime spree amounted to over a third of my total crime spree over 11 years by my 2.5ft deep police files .

That is over a 4 month period.

My social service records are blanked out up until the 27/02/81

This is when I answered the door to a social worker at the mount, why I really do not know, usually it was a house master who answered the door but my reports state that I answered the door to my social worker type woman (signed RGP on my reports), then they blank off the page again until the 06/03/81. (I wonder what I did in that 3 weeks to be blanked off like that??, but it happens many times throughout my files so I'm used to it by now and I don't seem to question it too much but some of the blanked off boxes later in St Gilberts home in Kidderminster home is bollox and is really getting to me as I could identify more my childhood accomplices if I knew who they were.

Don't ask about data protection and freedom of information, vie been through it all over the past few years whilst writing this, just don't go there.

Actually let's go there and have a rant at must be mid book.

Things I cannot mention as it's my word against there's.

I cannot mention social workers who transported me from place to place , homes to prison , , home to home , as they were not employed by the council so names are private , so that lets 2 pervs of the hook unless I press charges .

I cannot mention the names of the abusers in various homes due to the fact the relatives of the dead abusers could sue me as I have no proof that that happened, personally I would love to know if my relatives dead or alive were abusers if the evidence was in front of me, but alas I am not allowed, maybe 1day?. (99 years according to freedom of information)

I am not allowed to mention police officers due to the 2017 act where as an officer cannot be disciplined for an historic offence prior to dec 2012.

I am not allowed to mention the abused children in the homes, I understand that one fully.

A real narker for me is the freedom of information act , so much time to get your own files as it has to go through achieves ,then somewhere in a London office , then your own council (3 councils for me), I tell you what , it's a ball ache .

Near impossible to get all the files from the police, it takes months.

So let's jump to 03/03/81 SOCIAL ENQUIRY reports then if I can find them the SOCIAL WORKERS report... I found them

06/03/81 (RGP, Social workers report)

Timothy's case Number 2412/3.

Telephone call from Mr Stokes at the mount that timothy has absconded from school.

And returned home to Shrewsbury, Mrs. Draycott has phoned and agreed to put him on the bus back to school.

She said Timothy's reason for going to Shrewsbury was to pick up his football boots.

Mr stokes from the Mount feels that the increase in pressure from the O&a school to the manor school is giving timothy problems, I agreed to visit and bring him back - but nobody was in – C Stokes informed.

09/03/81 , (RGP) I rang Mr. stokes , Timothy returned at 7pm on the Friday and stayed the weekend at the mount , I agreed to call in on the Wednesday as timothy is anxious it seems about his forthcoming court appearance as he thinks he is going to get D.C (Detention centre).

11/03/81 , Visit to the mount , Mr Stokes and Mr Bellamy present ,they have agreed that the problems/truanting and absconding have arisen from the moving from belvidere to

vineyards to Hadley manor has an demanding effect on timothy ., other than that he has settled well in the days he has been present at the mount

(I need that social worker to decipher that – or can anyone tell me what a demanding effect is, it does not make sense).

Timothy seemed happy and cheerful but seemed worried and nervous about next week's court date

Oh come on RGP I don't understand that either, how could I be happy and worried and cheerful and nervous, this social worker was deffo a hippy.

I did a bunk once at the mount where I ended up at wellington station and thought its only a few miles to Shrewsbury I can walk the tracks of the railway lines , regardless of how I got to Shrewsbury as all I can think about is what I took back to the mount a few days later , but I remember the week before my court date I was going dolally thinking of what my brother was going through at borstal , I was about to be in the same boat in D.C , I was doing a bunk (Abscond) many times from the manor school , this is why I do not remember Hadley Manor to much as I was never bloody there .

My word I can tell you about some crime sprees back then from that school but they do not seem to be on my charge sheets and social services reports from these dates so I think I will have to bypass those stories, shame.

I will tell them stories if Angela Rippon comes back into talk show hosting, as she is lovely and gentle, but not the ex Sun newspaper bizarre's bloke Piers Morgan's life stories programme he did, as he will probably make me cry? Like he did with Sir Alan Sugar – that was funny or unless piers have legs like Angela I can stare at during the natter.

I have highlighted this short period of my life as I remember it quite well.

17/03/1981, (RGP)

Telephone call left for me that timothy has absconded yesterday from the mount (police have been informed).

18/03/1981 (RGP).

Checked with the mount and timothy returned 4pm that day on his own, A. Bellamy escorted him to school the following day .

20/03/1981.

Timothy attended court today and received a conditional discharge for 12 months and a £4 police fine, taken back to the vineyards (?) and all info passed to Mr. Bailey.

23/03/1981 & 24/03/1981 combined – to save space on the paragraph

Telephone call from the Mount Timothy has truanted again.

Telephone conversation with Mr stokes – he was obviously concerned with Timothy's behaviour since court and would like us to take him back to court – I said I didn't think we had grounds to do this but I would check and get back to him the following day.

Now let me rewind a bit here on my enquiry reports that state I arrived at the vineyards after court basically I didn't , I arrived at the mount as Mr C was present that day when I was dropped off , I was elated that I didn't get anything really at court but not so elated to see that grubby cunt sitting in the dining area laughing at me when I came in saying I would end up in prison for the rest of my life soon , sorry I have venom in me I must stop and compose myself .

Mr Stokes arrived the following day or so after court to berate me even more , fuck it , I did the same as I always did and run away from the situation , I could do a lot better in life (aged 14) , half of the staff at the Mount were dumbasses (in my view now) I either walked out of the front or back door or lifted up the shower room widow (that did not have the window stopper on it) to escape late at night .

I run away alone to Shrewsbury and stayed under the main railway station bridge a few times , I always felt it was closer to be home , in either direction of my hideouts where family I hopefully could rely on if I really needed (for them to get me back to institutilation probably).

So here we go on my confession to stealing from St Chad's church in Shrewsbury whilst rebelling against my poultry sentence.

My best friend at the time was a catholic , my family was split , I don't know why but I know a bit of the arguments that happened whilst I was signing forms in the police station throughout these years about was C of E , or Catholic , I said I was church of England , sometimes I said my dad was catholic , so I was catholic , (don't ask) I have no record but I know I said it many times in induction at youth custodies in the mid eighties , as i'm sure at the time Catholics got better treatment , not in medical terms , i mean recreation , watching T.V , dossing around more on a Sunday etc.

(o.m.g 25/05/20– armed police just tuned up in my street, (dead end street) 5 fast response police cars, 2 cop dog vans and a couple of unmarked police cars, they have surrounded a house 2 doors up and just screamed at me to go indoors as I am sitting in the sun in my front garden during this corona virus outbreak writing and reading, so this means I had to gather up all my paperwork and take inside – bloody loads of it aggh.

Bloody hell I'm nosy , so looking through my kitchen window down onto the neighbours front door (in not going into detail) I can see 6 police officers training guns on the door 2 doors down , 1 officer is constantly looking up at me as I look down to see what is going on , my laptop is on the window sill so I can be more of a nosey basterd , I remember all too well the abuse officers used to give out , but on this occasion I did not get out my camera or video as so many neighbours out to witness any wrong doings , I've just seen an officer load a round or something into his assault rifles chamber , I am literally 15ft from them as my flat is second floor , guns trained on the floor below , oooh no one seems to be in the house they are looking into .

Weird but I was knocking on the door this morning as I think they had post of mine.

So it all boils over, no one in, coppers don't know what to do so they are having a nice chat in their baklavas but staying 2m apart as they may catch Flu, personally I think we should have adopted herd immunity instead they have locked down the country, it would be nice to see what the outcome of Corona was in the future if your reading this in 2215 they are all leaving now but in drips and drabs.

 I have just spoken to an officer but he only wanted to know when the occupants left and if I have seen activity at the premises , "No" was my answer , as even though I totally respect them and believe in them (in later life I had donated marquees to my local police station for charity functions and even a car port so they could wash the police vehicles – I know – weird ,(if these current memoirs sell over 1204 paperback copies or 1,578 kindle copies you will know that info in my second memoir)

Personally I know the residents next door and below are a nice couple , they go about their business , she is a career in a home , he is a builder , I think they had the wrong address , so back to my story , sorry about that .

No, I'm off subject now so.

How can you tell the sex of an ant, place it in water

If it sinks ... girl ant

If it floats.....

Sorry for doing this but I'm going to take you back a touch.

The school which they sent me (Hadley manor , Telford)was not good for me , Mr (Mr Stokes, The Mount School , wellington) would give me bus fare daily to get to and from the school , most of the time it would go on chips from the Wellington or Oakengates chip shop and I would walk around or abscond back to Shrewsbury .

The school was massively in favour of boys over girls, around 70% boys and I thought at the time, this place is just full of mix raced pupils, you did not get this in Shrewsbury, and it was a major culture shock for me.

I had 1 black friend in Shrewsbury and I think he was the only black pupil in Belvidere and was liked by everyone.

Hadley Manor school I was constantly gobbed (spat) on whilst walking next to the school windows, I was kicked purposely whilst on Gym , lunch taken from in front of me in the dinner hall , it all happened here .

I had a fight in my 2nd week with a black lad they called waffle (not by me but by his friends) as his face was pitted with old acne, he was truly ugly in nature and looks (can he sue me for saying that?)

And fair play he did look like a Birdseye potato waffle (which are waffly versatile by the way – other top brand waffles which looked like his face are also available),what I thought was under my breath I called him something like crater face when he was picking on me in the hall ways to the classes , he lashed out with his foot (thinking he could do a kung foo kick like David Carradine) but in natural instinct and lucky for me I just managed to grab his foot ,(no violence intended) unlucky for me that he went off balance , fell back and banged his head on a classroom door , the same classroom door a teacher was in and about to walk out , came out with me standing over a full on moon face ,I think it happened that way , Waffle was a big big black lad who terrorised me constantly and hence the gobbing and future bullying from other black pupils .

I'm sure at that stage in my life I must have had plans for what I was going to do with my future , fireman , policeman , astronaut , car thief , I really do not know .

I also did not know any of my education whilst at Hadley manor , not a single thing ., I do not remember sitting in any classroom , I only remember the abuse I got .

Did I take R.E, geography, maths, English etc, I have not got a bloody clue and it is no reports I have received from the Telford councils.

Going back to the school majority of ethnic raced pupils has not had an effect on the rest of my life regarding racism as in my next home St Gilberts my best friend for 4 years was black , much more on junior later .

But as it stood life was not good at that moment in time, I remember so well the early eighties at the mount, and it was really not nice.

As mentioned I spent a total of 4–ish months at the Mount , reading reports from these 4 months , Mr stokes Really wanted to get shot of me , I do not know why but I suppose it came down to the amount of absconding I was doing , I'm sure I was not a trouble maker at the mount ?.

Shock to me and also maybe to you here is my crime spree for the months I was at the mount considering I was locked down after 5pm.

All that was the prologue, the book really starts here.

It was a cool dusky dank night and the birds were quiet with deathly laughter, or shall I start with "The warm moist air was cool to the touch as we approached the gates of Beelzebub ".

Oh I don't know, so let's jump straight in with.

We arrived at St Gilberts at lunch time to be met by no one. 19/06/1981

(*From now on nearly all names have been changed to protect the guilty*).

We went in through the front door , around the ground floor , into the dining area then up the dominating stairs , wow them stairs where very wide , very wooden and the carpet was plushly centered (plushly centered , where did that come from ? , do them words actually exist , yes in my brain they do) So showing the wooden steps either side of it.3484

The wall paper was equally amazing, it was red patterned in the form of fleur de Lys, but all the fleur de Lys in red felt with a dark cream background, that must have cost a bloody small fortune as a roll of that when I looked into it back in the 90s was around £60 a roll.

From ground floor to ceiling in the main stair way was around 70ft , the stairs dominated inside the main entrance , I remember them so well as I used to slide down the banister , I will see if I can find an non copyrighted photo (I doubt I thought).

The stairs stopped at the middle floor , (white windows in the photo above) a large balcony looked over to the ground floor but mainly just the bottom of the large stairs , you could see the main door from these stairs , then the stairs started again to go to the top floor , (main door then hidden) another balcony going to the left of the stairs , which led to my first room at St Gilberts , to the right and left of the stairs were dormitory rooms.

My room was along a long corridor, second door on the right just at the top of 5 steps going down to 2 other doors (you will see the drop in the building in the photo on the top left), the ceiling in this corridor was high, very very high.

As I looked up I seen an attic hatch – one thing to note for the future as I was planning escape routes on my first day , that's if I didn't like the place.

I shared the room with 2 others but room enough for at least 8 beds; my bed was by the window, unlike the Mount these windows opened fully.

I recently visited St Gilberts and there is no way of getting to it to take photos , it is completely surrounded by new build houses and a gated entrance , it's like they are trying to hide what went on in their ?, Hiding the building so no one can see it , the building is a ghost , (to me it does anyway) .

Right, let's go for this –probably no full stops.

The first few days as with all Homes were a bit hair raising, meeting all the staff and future abused lads (no girls).

The names of the pupils are not allowed to be mentioned in my reports but I remember every lad in there (first and last name)names I can never forget as I classed them as best friends , we did everything together , please ....read on .

Wolseley farm was my first physical contact with a member of staff around a week into me being settled in at the home.

I think the farm belonged to a local man and the home used to help out and for educational purposes, literally 100 yards at the rear the main house.

Cows, sheep, chickens, I cannot recall any sheep though?

The Chicken shed I cleaned was massive , 10 thousand broiler chicks every few months , the rate of growth was amazing , 1 day you would go in and chicks , the next time they would be half chicken size , then the sudden spurt of growth .

Half way through the growth we would have to shovel the shit, o.m.g, the smell of ammonia was so over powering, we had to wear a mask, the shit was either hard as nails due to the walking on by the chicks and then you would get a squidgy patch which was just the worst experience to shovel, we would make 4ft piles by the door and the tractor would come and shovel it up.

"Wanna suck my dick", wow that was a shocker from a house master? I had just met, "No "I think was the simplest answer I gave

"Go on, I know what goes on in the (those) dorms and I know that you suck dick".

(I think there is a pattern in this going to homes thing , 3 homes in 4 so far housemasters wanted to be sucked , was I that ugly that that they didn't want to go down on me ? (But that would change soon).

I said no a few times to that perv on that farm on that day in the chicken shed.

On that particular day I remember he kept looking outside whilst I was shovelling shit and coming back up to me saying no one was coming and if we are quick we could get away with it .

This was in my first couple of weeks, the bloke did not even try to groom me, he just wanted his dick sucked, not just on that occasion but a few, and always down the farm.

Now this one is a difficult one for me as I do not remember his name, I have no memory of his name, I do know what he looks like but his name does not spring out on any reports.

It makes me upset that I do not know his name and I try to think too much about him as he is the only man I could not identify on paper , maybe I do not want to remember his name and it has be blanked from my memory , so we will have to bypass that armpit smelly tosser.

Sometimes I think he may have been a farm hand who dressed well and took charge of us whilst we were down the farm, he also asked me whilst when we went pheasant beating in shooting season, I vaguely recall in the coups they had in the woodlands him asking me but I could be wrong, why mention it then, I don't know.

I'm over thinking again so I must stop.

(that was a shit job , beating the bushes in farmed woodlands so the pheasants flew up for the posh tweed jacket types to shoot , at the end of the day they the farmers would give us 10 embassy regal untipped fags (cigarettes), a small can of Mackeson stout ale which we had to drink there and some pheasants to take back to St Gilberts ,("oh come on I was 14ish, ffs ") then they would take us back to the home in a beat up land rover with braces of pheasants stinking and bleeding in the back with us , we were filthy and stinking of blood).

Enough of that bloke as I cannot recall his name which is still annoying and upsetting me after trying to rest from this book for a few weeks, in this time I have visited London, Bristol, Brighton, Somerset coastline and even the gates of the farm to St gilberts to think and make notes of my next chapters and I still can't think of his name?.

"Can I suck your dick Tim ", whaaaaat, wow that was a surprise.

That was the voice of one of my fellow interns, same age as me within the first few weeks.

In the dorm room, late at night, one other in the room.

"No I'm ok "I said, then an almighty laugh came from the other side of the room from our fellow roommate (I remember both lads names very well).

We laughed about it , fellow roommate was saying that he really wanted to do it whilst other was egging him on to come and do it , I was telling them about the abusers I have encountered and they were saying I must of had my dick sucked in that time .

A few hours later that night I awoke to my roommate sucking my dick, he had crept alongside my bed and fair play to the lad got the right angle to attack my cock.

I remember our other roommate laughing and I think that woke me more than the dick sucking did, he got up and asked if I could do the same to him, "eh No way ", roommate still laughing and shouting in a quiet voice "ha ha you been sucking his dick "

Cock sucking Roommate was in denial saying we were chatting but the other roommate would have none of it saying he seen him creeping up on all fours to my bed, he told me so many times what he had done, I had no reason to disbelieve him as I was hard when I woke up, I dread to think how long he was doing it for and the other roommate was probably getting a kick out of watching him going down on me?.

I did not know if I enjoyed it or not as I was asleep and caught him half way down my cock.

(O.m.g this is getting to be a porn novel now, I dread to think what I was dreaming at the time)

Dick sucking roommate asked me on a few occasions throughout the years at St Gilberts if he could go down on me and I am definitely going to tell you about this later in this year and the following years chapters. *(Why, because it's funny)*

I have more paperwork from April 1981- October 1984 whilst at St Gilberts, far play to them they kept many notes and I am so happy for it.

Every trip or outing is here, every absconding adventure, every name or every abuser.

And the bonus is that I still have photos of my time here with the pupil's names on the back of the photos, I do not need them but it helped a bit.

I stole a newly brought out disc camera by Kodak, the film was expensive so I stole them as well, I had to pay for developing, they all wanted to play with it , but the photos will be later

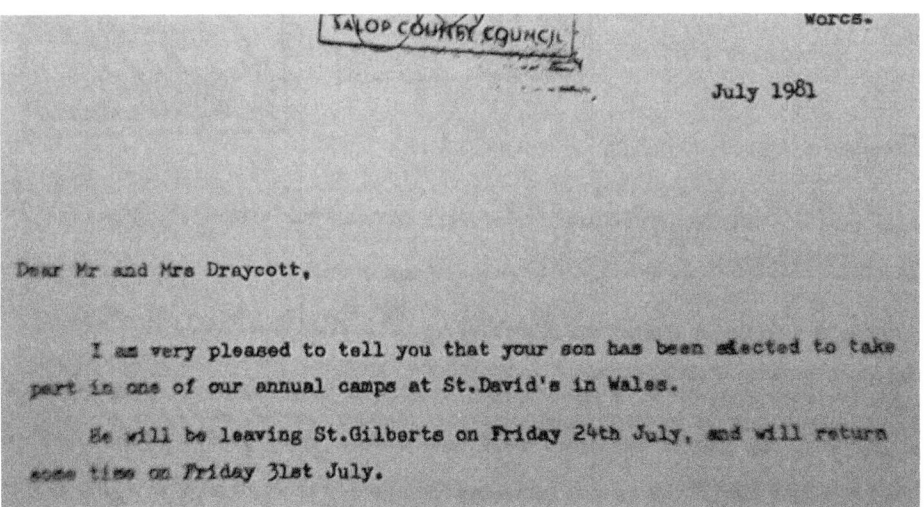

SALOP COUNTY COUNCIL   worcs.

July 1981

Dear Mr and Mrs Draycott,

    I am very pleased to tell you that your son has been elected to take part in one of our annual camps at St.David's in Wales.

    He will be leaving St.Gilberts on Friday 24th July, and will return some time on Friday 31st July.

I don't remember that, I wonder what I did there.

Let's get back to the farm and sticking my arm up a cows arse, no I think we will not go there at the moment as I have just found the Machynlleth camping trips reports of my behaviour, so I'm going to tell you about our visit to the centre for alternative technology.

On some occasions the home would take us out to various destinations in the country as part of our learning and the housemasters grooming time.

We stayed at a local camping site just out of town , the loveliest of loveliest farmers daughters was at the house every year and we struck up a little kissing relationship in the farm out buildings , by the stream (to which there was many)until ...

A French students party arrived the same time as us , we got on well , the language was difficult as we did not learn French , I did learn a touch at Belvidere , un , der , twar , catra , sank , Sikh ,wept , un table catra sank , something like that .

I perfectly understood the "me no baby, me no baby "as I wanted to enter a French girl I managed to get back to my tent.

Whoa, I'm not getting into this porn thing again so I will simply say this is the first ever girl I entered without using my winky todger as she would have none of it.

Her hands pushing my todger way " me no baby , me no baby " goes through my head so many times , I did say to her in a sign language that I would take it out before I ejaculated

(circled thumb and finger with a finger going in and out) , but she still would have none of it , I got to do other things but alas I was still a virgin .

The following morning it was the talk of the campsite due to Paul looking in the tent and catching us and then my little blond haired kissing girlfriend dumped me. (I never seen frenchie again as they packed up quick and did a bunk early)

After the second year we never went back to that campsite, blondes mother found out and banned the boy's home from visiting again. *(Lol)*

I have passed the lane leading to the farm many many times and I often wonder if my kissing blonde girlfriend still lives here , would she remember me ? , she was stunning, would she still go out with me now I'm 52? I doubt it so let's carry on.

A file which is to large will not fit on this page so here is an empty space , you can use this empty space to reflect on life , whats happening around you , phone a family member or go make a cup of tea xx , im going to use it to think of what my t-shirts would look like if my washing machine had not of broken down.

St.Gilbert's Boys' School,
Hartlebury,
Kidderminster,
Worcs.

NAME: **Timothy Wayne DRAYCOTT**

Period in school: Six months

     Good

Comment on health:

Date: 11.12.81

Age: 14.9

Unit: Kinver

RESIDENTIAL SOCIAL WORK REVIEW REPORT

Timothy has been with Kinver since being admitted to St.Gilberts and has settled down quite well in this unit. He is respectful of his surroundings and is a pleasant, helpful boy to have around. For the most part he does not present many behavioural problems and works well at the targets on his card. He was the first boy to go straight from a basic card onto a weekly card in the Token Economy system and his present targets are:

     1. No teasing.
     2. Friendly involvement with peers.
     3. Classroom behaviour

The major problem that has evolved since Tim arrived is his tendency to run from the unit when upset.

He usually uses his leisure time to good effect playing squash regularly and being involved in most activities offered. When having time to spare in the unit he has shown an interest in making and painting models of cars.

Tim relates well to adults and has formed a particular bond with one male member of the team. We feel this is significant as his history suggested that relationships, other than with his mother, have always been kept at a superficial level. He is generally very co-operative but at times becomes a nuisance by repeating requests that have already been refused or are irrelevant. Because his inappropriate attention seeking takes more than a reasonable amount of staff time Tim is in danger of missing out on attention he is due when needing to discuss more important matters.

Tim has not formed a close friendship with any one boy. He tends to be on the fringe of the group, but he is accepted by everyone. At times he presents himself as a timid boy within the unit which leaves him open to being pressured by the stronger personalities.

Home contact has been regular, but has recently become more problematic because of his not returning to school on time on several occasions without real excuse: missing the bus or train. On returning from home leave he has always said how much he has enjoyed the weekend.

Timothy has shown anxiety before court appearances and at this time has become unsettled in school showing a tendency to abscond or run off with little explanation. With no more court appearances in sight, other than his deferred sentence hearing, we hope this behaviour will not recur.

In summary, this is Tim's first review at St.Gilberts and the only obvious problems he needs to work on are his tendency to run off when under stress rather than going to adults for help and his inappropriate attention seeking. He should be encouraged in his special relationship without being allowed to become over dependent. If he continues to keep out of serious trouble and goes on co-operating he should improve on the already good reports he has gained.

Some points on the above, Kinver Unit was the main building and they are lying when they said I was childish.

Everything else I think I have to agree on, I don't want to but I suppose I must.

A.Gilbert's Boys' School,
Hartlebury,
Kidderminster

NAME: Timothy DRAYCOTT   Date: 11.12.81

Date of birth: 10.3.67   Age: 14.5   Date of admission: 5.6.81

Class/Vocational Unit: Teacher:

Educational attainments   Class 1   Mr.N.Davies

Reading: years   Test:

Arithmetic: Oral age.....................) NFS test of
               Mechanical age...............) arithmetic
               Full scale...................) competence

CLASSROOM REPORT

English: Tim works well in these lessons, he does however, resist suggestion
preferring to plan his own output. This is usually in the form of story writing of
some length. His spelling and sentence construction are of a good standard.
Timothy chooses his own reading material from the class library.   MB

Maths: Tim usually works well during these lessons, at least for 90 minutes, the other
minutes he fills by doodling and being silly - Please, Tim, the time for playing is
passed and you must use every minute of your time to improve the standard of your
work which you are quite capable of doing.   KT

Art: Timothy can produce some very good work but needs constant assurance that he is
doing well etc. This can be rather tiresome ! His approach to acquiring materials
for his work is almost infantile - this is one area where he could start to develop
maturely.   TC

Geography: Tim shows a keen interest in all the work we do. His map and written work
are always well presented.   CY

PE/Games: If he committed himself fully to the tasks at hand I am sure Tim would
reach a standard far greater than he has reached so far. Often his mind is on other
things. He enjoys playing squash and is improving slowly in basketball.   ND

Child care: Tim shows a keen interest in this subject and is willing to discuss
points at length. His attitude towards his peers is good and he can argue a point
sensibly.   CT

Classteacher:

Many comments in Tim's weekly diary refer to his silly behaviour. It seems he needs
to pull himself together and concentrate on the task at hand, rather than
displaying disruptive tactics.

CONCLUDING COMMENTS

     For a good deal of his time Tim works well but there are still too many instances
of silly disruptive behaviour. If Tim is to reach anything like his full potential
he must realise that the time for playing is over and hard work is the only
alternative.

Silly behaviour my ass.

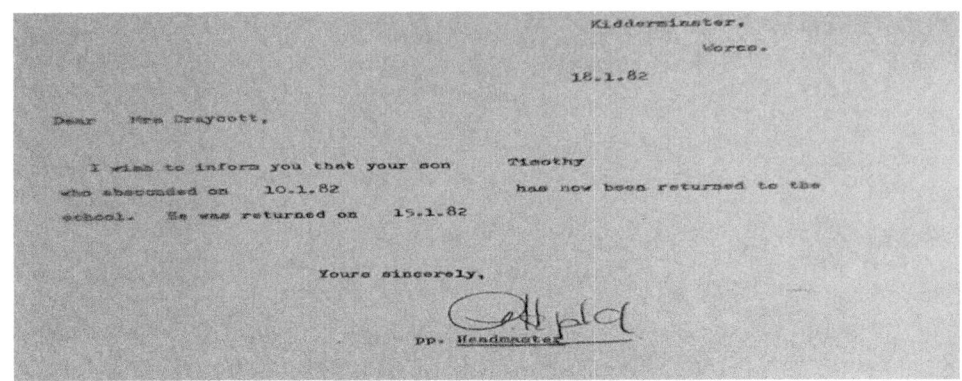

Weather wise If you thought beast of the east was bad back in 2018 , when you are 15 years old you would not think cold would really effect you but on the night of the 10/11th January 1982 – wow it affected me in a big way .

I really needed to escape from St Gilberts and this was the ideal time, no one would expect a breakout in this weather, if I get something in my head to do I must follow it through.

(Still applies today).

I told a couple of lads in the dorm , Andy and Paul what I was doing , I can't remember the words but they thought I was nuts to go out , but that was my way then I must run away .

Junior was asleep so I nicked his new Dr martins 18 lace hole , I was size 7 , junior was size 9 or 10 (I told you he was big in many ways , or did I yet ?) , I had to put 5/6 pairs of socks on to make them fit ok , just as well really .

I had on my person or stuffed in the pockets – 2-ish jumpers on , 2-ish t-shirts on, 5-ish pairs socks on , 1 large hooded jacket on , 1 pair jeans on (maybe 2 pairs) , 1 pyjama bottoms on , stolen damps (fag butts with a bit of tobacco on them) from staff ashtray downstairs ,

(even though I did not smoke yet) kitchen size matches , smallest pen knife in the whole wide world (I mean that) , biscuits , milk , a couple of star wars toys which I knew where keepers which I lost later anyway , I probably took more but I knew that I was stacked and sweating before I even left the building .

So started my journey , I'm thinking as this is going to go on for some time (probably with no full stops)maybe you should get yourself a cup of tea or a nice craft ale (look online for Salopian brewers and order some proper stuff – no plug intended).

I will wait here for a minute and start after the full stop.

St Gilberts was great for escape as so many doors, so many corridors and rooms to hide in if staff is having a nose late at night.

So I made my escape through the rear of the house looking on to the farm 100yrds away.

I took a route through fields enroute to the Kidderminster area , knowing that I would pick up the railway lines that would take me directly to Kiddy , I have past them a few times in some sort of car , you had to go near a railway bridge (A449 meets A450 on the Worcester Rd), that's when tony Simcoe took the tumble into the fish pond , so I knew I was doing the right thing in going this way and pre planning my route for this way .

This "right" thing was happening in the worst snow weather since the 1950s and regardless of beast of the east snow in the uk in 2018 (I was driving up through Spain at that time in my motor home during beast of the east, we had it bad in Madrid 2018, I was snowed in Spain before the uk was – really weird).

So I managed to find the railway line that would take me past Hartlebury station and onto kiddy , I was freezing but also sweating as I just trundled through countless farmers fields , the snow drifts in some places where like the east side of the Eiger (Just to let you know I have never been to the east side of the Eiger) I had to stay in the middle of the fields as most impossible along the hedge rows , it was a light sky at night , maybe a full-ish moon but I had to risk it , I had to take a jumper off due to the sweat but my toes where freezing , the boots caused no problems walking apart from that I had to raise them higher to get through the snow and the things weighed a tonne and stupidly I put them on really tight , considering the layers I had on my tootsies I thought it would cause me no problems , I was wading through up to 3 feet of snow for up to 2 miles before I decided the feet were too cold to carry on and I must investigate what the problem was , I nearly died on that line , no seriously I was that cold I thought this is it , no cover , no heat , no nothing really .

This was by far the worst absconding trip I had ever done, yes even worse than seeing a young Scottish lad being beaten up in Glasgow.

This rail line just went on and on with no bridges to shelter under, at one stage I did think about giving up and making a fire under a tree but I was only 2-ish miles into my journey, I still had another 4ish miles to go before I could steal some decent sort car to get me to Shrewsbury but first I knew I had to cross the bridge.

Yes the bridge, the dreaded Bridge, at that given time my nemesis, the bridge.

This railway bridge is big , very big , very big and tall and I have to either walk over it or under it , now going under it was dangerous as 4 main route roads cross underneath it and a hot spot for coppers , always to be avoided , so my best route was on it .

I understand now after retracing my footsteps in various places that they have a dedicated path for this bridge and low and behold it's called the railway path, that's the path I should have taken back in 1982 but I'm sure it was not there then, what was there under the bridge was the chippy (fish and chip shop) underneath the Viaduct which I later when in the Kidderminster college studying retail distribution I come to use as my local chippy.

I came to the start of the bridge and basically nearly shat myself, (it would have been ok as the shit would have been like ice cubes) the bridge on top was deep in snow and all I seen in front of me was a pure white path and 150ft below roads and buildings, you could not see either side of the bridge, and to this day I do not know the height of the wall on the bridge.

(Just done research, so you don't have to, it is a 20 arch, 371 yard (339M) long,

75ft (23M high), 7 million bricks , total cost to build £30,000 which weirdly enough was the total damage I caused to Underdale rd ,Sankeys warehouse I burnt down a few years before)

I know it's not for pedestrians to walk across this viaduct but I took the bold step to walk across and just follow the white 20ft wide path , yeah more difficult than I though .

The snow on the bridge came up to my tits and at that time I must have been 4ft, I had to keep in 1 straight line, it felt an eternity and when I got to the other side it was most impressive looking back on my wading marks through the snow in between the 2 sets of tracks, the wall was approx 3ft high. Eeeek when I think back.

(I should have been bear griylls as some of the places I stayed in or at and looked after myself are unbelievable, and yes if you are the questiony sort, I have skinned rabbit, plucked game, gutted and castrated pigs & piglets, sheep, even winkles and duck, stuck my arm up a cows ass once (yuk), milked goats and drove a trac-teerrr.

All before the age of 15.

I found a railway carriage attached to a row of train container type things only a few hundred yards later after the bridge, this carriage was at the rear of the train which must have been at least a million feet long but as I had crossed the bridge I had to either find a car to steal in this weather at around 2am or snuggle down and see what the situation was with my feet.

The carriage must have been perfect, it was around 30ft long, and it had a fire stove in the centre and benches running either side of the carriage, Bonus

I took my boots of and found I had lost 4 toes to frostbite.

Ha, only joking about the toes, (Just *trying to make the book dramatic*).

I tore up some wood from a locker and lit a fire in the stove, it was still cold, I vaguely remembering me drinking a hot drink or beans in this carriage but I have stayed in other train carriages in Shrewsbury so I may be mistaken but I know I woke up very early at first light so I must have been knackered to fall asleep in that cold.

(Just remembered , Beans in a can over a fire happened on the church Stretton to Shrewsbury railway line in a 4ftx4ft railway side hut , when I was about 12/13 and at Besford house .- I sometimes hate these memory flashes , but its good) .

I stole a Morris minor just after the bridge (but level with the bridge top, if you know what I mean) as they were by far the easiest to steal with my pocket pen knife, and that type of car was in abundance if you looked in the right areas, I did not want to make a noise with a ford or a vw and to find a scaffold pole to break the steering lock off in that weather was nigh on impossible.

(Oh - them town areas as I mentioned for (moggy) Morris minors to be stolen from where mainly older houses in terraces , near to towns , very rare to find them on housing estates , new built housing estates means -nearly new cars , posh housing estates – new cars , etc etc

etc) ,I strike it lucky by finding one on a main street leading into the town , I did not have to drive through the ring road of kiddermister , I just had to double back to the Bromsgrove road and go up towards wolves to get home .

The car had no heating , typical , the windows iced up as soon as you put the flimsy blowers on , I had to open the sliding door window to clear the inside window as it was frosting up pretty damn fast ,(my heart goes out to you Mr Peary) it was like that until I ran out of fuel near Bridgnorth .

Sorry to say I do not have anything on my crime sheets or reports to say what I stole that night to carry on my journey another 18ish miles to Shrewsbury .

I know it's not the night I stole the fz50cc moped , that was in thick snow but I really cannot see me riding that thing from Bridgnorth to Shrewsbury on " that" road , in " That" weather

I don't think it was the night when I broke into the car dealer garage at bridgenorth as I remember the siding doors had no obstruction and I'm sure 5-6ft of snow drifts would have blocked that door.

So we must put this down to, (as it's not on my reports), that I walked, yes that's it. I walked, honest; maybe it was the cold as it was minus something.

On the 14th I was found in Shrewsbury and placed in the Mount in wellington on the 15th until St Gilberts fetched me (which was supposed to be that day according to reports).

This was not a nice experience as I had only just left that punishment chamber, the abuse I got from Mr was more than abuse , he locked me in a room with Old Christmas decorations boxes , that fucking massive fake 70s Christmas tree that hardly had any needles on it and worst of all , no window , he told me I would be getting a good hiding later , he said he never did like me , my family where all scum on the dole and I will end up like my dad and brother , pushed me violently against the boxes and left me there until late at night .

Late night came and I was out of there like a shot , I followed what the housemaster did and went through the fire hatch into the adjoining dorm , out the door ,through the kitchen window to freedom , I don't know what happened then or what I did but I was to be returned to St Gilberts on the 19th from the mount school , they held a review for me at St Gilberts whilst I was on the run , on the 18th whilst I was probably stealing a car somewhere in thick snow in Shrewsbury ?.

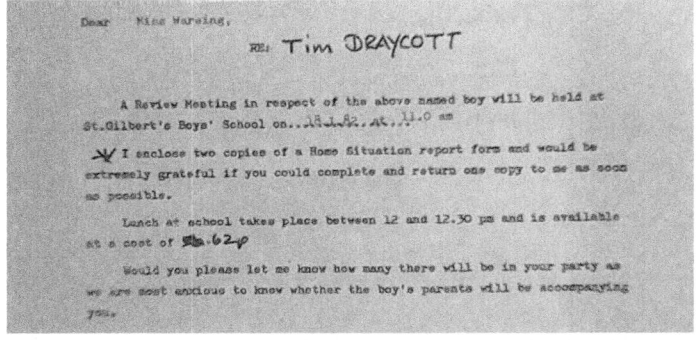

My February reports seem quite quiet and it seems I settled back into St Gilbert's life.

Basket ball was on the sports agenda quite a lot for me at St Gilberts, it was strenuous but I plugged away at it , (*according to reports I still preferred comics apparently*) but slightly later in life Basketball and squash would be a big part of my life , (*a very big part*).

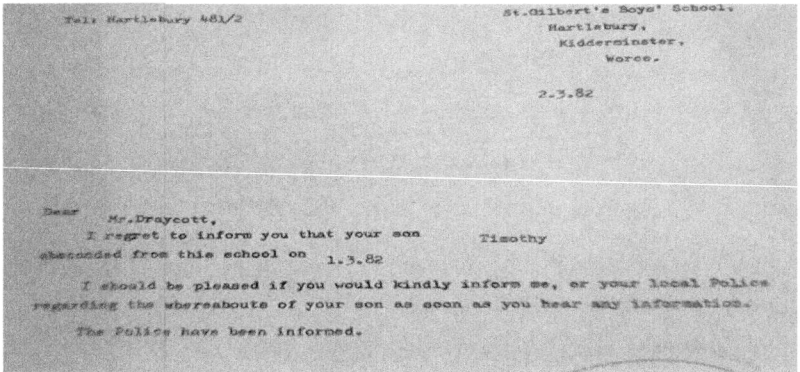

Tony Simcoe (Dodd) my old chum from Besford house and throughout my early years came to pick me up one night at St Gilberts, (we still kept in touch when I returned home for holidays and weekends, it was the early days of St Gilberts a few days before my birthday and a week before my biggest ever court date, I knew as I could drive then and I had only been driving for a year.

I do not recall the meeting with tony or the escape from the bastillion but I do remember me in the area of Hartlebury meeting tony he had done a bunk/runner from Besford house and I did a runner from St Gilberts, we must have pre arranged on a weekend home when I would usually go to Besford anyway to meet friends.

This would not be the first triumph 1300 that I stole, they were very easy to steal, desirable now but back then they were classed as shit.

Tony drove an escort Mk2 with square headlights which I thought was weird at the time I suppose as I have stolen many a ford escort with round headlights , this was new to me and I was excited about it all , I Wanted his car instead of my soft top crap .

He stole this from Telford and as no ANPR back in these days you could drive anywhere as long as you have the cushion under your bum.

We arranged to meet somewhere, I really do not know where and I am sure it does not matter either but Tony sped off, I had to put on the chase.

Around 4 miles away from the boys Home is a very tricky bend and I think you know what I am about to say ...

The bend is an S chicane, and in the middle of the S on the left is a pond approx 40ft round, deep I did not know?

(Since revisiting this pond I can now happily say it is 60ft long, 30ft wide and approx 6ft deep, covered in algae and a lot more trees around it now)

I came around this corner at no more than 40mph (35kph) at 10-11pm to see Tones car sinking in the pond and what I thought was the tail lights just about to go under the water.

Oh dear me I probably thought, I stopped a hundred yards away on the kerb, when I ran back he was sitting next to the pond looking a bit worse for wear, everything was wet and half a ford escort was sticking out of the pond, the front fully submersed up to the front window, oh dear I probably thought again.

It was not too late and cars were still going past so we hightailed it to my car , in front of my car was another car and an old man walking towards us from it " are you ok , how old are you 2 "

"Fuck off" was the only answer tony was willing to give and all I remember as I started to laugh and then he jumped in the driving seat of my car the twat.

The man then carried on walking to the submarine car whilst looking at me trying to talk tony into giving me my car back.

The old man came back to talk to me and as I am a nice polite lad I spoke to him , I told him I was from St gilberts the private school up the road and this is my father's car and that's my brother ," we have stopped to see if that car is in trouble ".

And then he told me he was the car behind tony when it went in the pond and he had to go turn around to see if the driver was ok   , I suppose I was looking silly at that time giving a blatant lie to a stranger.

Tony came back out of the car and told me to get in which I did whilst tony was ranting at the old bloke to mind his own business, I think he knew what we were about as he gave up talking to us and going to the sunken car and went back to his car mumbling under his breath, Time to hightail it as a phone box was just down the road, but the nearest police station would be 8 miles away in Kidderminster giving us 10 mins to get out of there.

We passed a couple of coppers on the way to the Kidderminster area , old man must of phoned 999 , but tony was taller than me , it was dark , so they just sped past us .

I really do not know the rest of the journey so I will have to stop there and have a cup of tea, read more reports, more files, and more bullshit from social services saying how bad I was.

But hey ho I have come to this part in March 82 which I'm sure everyone praises me no end.

I've just read the next bit of my police/court and social services reports and they do not praise me.

08/03/82 social services report

Just received a phone call from Shrewsbury police , timothy arrested 06/03/82 and has been held in custody charged with taking and driving , burglary etc , due to appear in a special juveniles court at 10am , same day , Case finally heard at 3.30pm , 3 months detention centre .

March 1982, the start of my adult life chapter

OH my word , the juvenile court dates for march 1982 don't seem right , I'm sure I was convicted for around 15-20 crimes as the mage was just reeling them off a sheet of paper that went through the doorway , (*that was a slight exaggeration*)but it says here 10 , 4 brought forward from November 81.

I must have admitted to more in the writing off crimes if I admit to one, good for the crime stats in the 80s and I'm sure it has not changed.

08/03/81, juvenile court (2 days before my 15th Birthday)

Court No 1, sorry 12 crimes not 10.

Criminal damage , this was the spray painting of Woolworths front window shop , I stole the spray from Halfords next door in Shrewsbury and started to spray my name on the window, I know why .. Don't go there.

Burglary , theft , taking conveyance without authority , driving no insurance , driving no licence , oooh and thrown in was a burglary and theft of a dwelling , oh shit I've just turned the page on my files and found more (so this knocks the tally up).

Aiding and abetting driving whilst disqualified, burglary, more taking and driving away, Theft.

This brings it up to 23 court offences for the first few months at The Mount School in wellington before I left.

Only a couple of these crimes were committed at St Gilberts in the first month, them being the car thefts in January and early march.

I remember the magistrate in the court so well, the smug look on her face when she said the crimes I have committed have given this town a bad name in the local news as I (apparently dominated it with my antics, the bloke on the left looked like a oversized hamster, the women on the right of the main magistrate was a snooty old lady who was more interested in looking directly at me throughout the hearing.

"I'm sending you down, 6 months detention centre, to run concurrent with other offences "and so she rabbited on mentioning all what I had done and how many concurrents there where

I was Numb , I didn't hear a lot thereafter as I started to cry in the dock and cry a lot I did , in fact I was bawling uncontrollably , no mother to comfort me over the brass bars separating public from crook , being stared at by everyone , I knew no one , all I was thinking about was what my brother had said to me when he went to borstal , borstal , it's bad , don't go there .

social report - *Mrs Draycott was at the police station looking for Tim whilst he was in court, whilst Sheryl was left alone at home , we will have to address this at a later date but before April 1st (?)*What did they mean by that I wonder?

was lucky in that borstal was now no more and they changed the Name to detention centre, borstal was getting a bad name for brutality by the prison officers to inmates and it was known to be an army style regime.

The Criminal justice act abolished borstals in early 1982, making room for detention centres, basically the same but a name change.

The name Borstal came about from the village of Borstal where the first Borstal was built.

Good bit of education for you, you can have that one for free.

did not want to go , I tried to run away from the court twice that same hour , they locked me in a court side room whilst waiting for the police , the old market hall in Shrewsbury is really not cut out to be a court house , only 1 real way in , apart from the magistrates have their own private door , they have to climb stairs to get to the back of the court house , we go up stairs to the small waiting room , the building was tiny and still is but I think now a 100 seat cinema is up in the old market hall now .

The room they locked me in was at least 30ft from street level , I opened the window and attempted to get out to the roof (it was closer than the floor)but was apprehended by my solicitor who talked me down and when the police arrived and took me downstairs to the police van , like my father did 20 years previously I pushed the copper away and tried to hightail it with cuffs on but soon (within 4 steps) I was caught , I cried in the van , I cried in the police station , on the way to Eastwood park detention centre and in reception of Eastwood park detention centre .

Falfield, a tiny little place in the middle of know where down the M5 motorway, 2 hours drive from Shropshire, approx 120 miles, Gloucester

had travelled further but this seemed the longest journey of my life, cuffed as I was an absconder, "For Petes sake I'm a juvenile, you can't treat me like this".

Chapter, Err...This one.

think this journey is where I really became an adult ,(on my way to a real prison) everything in life prior to this I would get away with as I was a juvenile , oooh no not this time , time to grow up .

This is a bit difficult for me as I have very limited files to go with the 2 detention centres I went to in the same year , I have the social workers reports for when he/she visited , they did not do a weekly log on you here (*I have requested but I'm far too late , as they were destroyed 20 years ago*) so I have to go by memory alone , as I do not remember to much I can only say what I know and remember , I really wish it was more

So I hope you do not mind I am going to combine them together as I do recollect which was which , I knew that I was an orderly in both so that gives me a start .

I hope you understand the combining of prisons as it felt like one continuous sentence (3 month difference, basically I was out for 3 months).

WELCOME TO EASTWOOD PARK, BIIIIIG sign at the entrance said.

I'm not going to beat around the bush on this one , the reception area was long and thin , the screws shouted at me every step I took , they made me strip , they looked up my bottom (only on 1 occasion) , they gave me a square bundle of blue clothes ,a bed pack perfectly folded together then they marched me down a long corridor (called the M1) .

When I say marched it was marched, I was told how to do this in the reception area whilst keeping my arms straight holding the bed & clothes pack (that hurt).

Everything was centred on the M1, the sports hall, the dining room, the long corridor wings leading to the cells, the laundry and basically everything else, (I wonder if it is still called the M1).

Don't forget I did say in the prologue that my grammar was terrible so please bear with me.

The screw (sorry prison warden) walked me down this long corridor, the flooring throughout the building was amazing, you could see your face in the floor tiles on the M1, it felt like a 10 minuets walk just to walk down the M1, very very intimidating but I had to do this journey to get to my ensuite room, I could feel eyes on me every step of the way with other "prisoners" looking through the small windows of each cell at me when nearing my destination.

I have no real thoughts of this long walk , I think I would have lost all my tears by this time , knew I had to be brave and I'm not sure but any human being would regret the crimes they had done walking down this mirror floored prison but to be honest I remember so well at my first detention centre I had no remorse for the crimes I had committed ,I think I committed more crimes in detention centre than I did outside in the real world , this place is going to be a big learn for me , I got taught by the older generation here how to steal properly , my second visit I was the teacher .

The screw just pointed to get in the room, I don't think we shared 1 word from reception to ensuite room; we just marched, just like I was told to do from the reception officers.

Ensuite room my ass , it was a fuckin cell , 10ft x 8ft approx , (sorry not researched but that is my size estimate) , it had a bed , a cupboard highly graphitized with a flip up table attached and a piss stained potty , oh and a window , let's not forget the window as it plays a massive part of my early prison life in the latter stages of detention centre , it had 4 pane of glass missing from the 80 or so small glass pains in a 5ft x 5ft window , you could just get your arm out .

6.30am on the button a giant captains bell started to ring , the noise that followed was horrendous , the clattering of doors being unlocked , the sounds of hundreds of inmates waking up and shouting at each other , no one came out of the cells .

I sat up in my sodden wet through bed.

I did peep out of the door but was told to get my neck in and stay in by a burly screw at the end of the cell wing; I did as I was told.

After around 15 minutes another bell sound and then the almighty sound doors banging closed and then of hundreds of feet walking down the corridors – marching.

Oh shit, I'm not going to like this place, I was shitting myself.

I shit myself more on the second time as I knew what was about to come.

A screw came to my door with an inmate, he directed him to teach me how to do a bed pack, and he gave me an induction form and a sheet of A4 with timings and rules of the detention centre.

You did not get any of this on your second visit, straight into work the following day

This bed and clothes pack had to be perfectly square and to be done every morning, we had 15 mins from bell 1 to bell 2 to get up, fold precisely the bed linen and clothes into 1 pack.

This had to be placed on the bed on the naked mattress, the potty had to be scrubbed clean (I had to scrub someone else's dried on piss off the plastic potty), boots and shoes polished and us standing inside the door standing to attention, ready to be inspected.

That was a typical wake up, then stand outside your door after you have been inspected by the head of the wardens.

We would get marked on the quality of our bed pack, if the bed pack was not good enough you would do extra choirs in the prison.

On that occasion I did not get caught wetting the bed as the screw left me with the inmate to teach me, he was ok and we struck up a friendship which lasted the 3 and a bit months I was inside for (I have now forgotten his name), he arrived 1 day prior to me, the following day I taught 3 new inmates to fold bed packs, so that was the norm, new inmates teach new inmates.

Not the second time though as you went straight into the regime of obedience.

After the wake up we are frog marched to the canteen, where approx 300 inmates are eating at the same time, my first experience of a prison tray, separated compartments on a thin metal tray.

The slop what got dumped on it was quite mad in the morning , porridge , a bit of jam if you're lucky from the measly bowl of it at the end of the line , a slice of toast , cornflakes with a small ladle of milk ,no sugar but inmates brought some along in a little folded handmade envelope – they didn't share .

Weekends are better as we are treated to an egg or a sausage or even a slice of dried bacon, the tea in the urn was always stewed, (it was rank), we had a big plastic cup which was chewed or cracked, we had to keep this cup throughout our intern but the trays got washed by hand by inmates, sometimes not very good as you would often find remnants of the previous meal stuck to the tray.

I have to mention the Duff , this is a large sponge square (approx 4"x4"), every prison , youth custody I have been to serve Duff , mainly it was lemon sponge or a funny pink colour sponge to represent ... Just a pink colour I think , the unsugared custard was poured in abundance over it .

O.m.g , I can taste it now , me shovelling it in the mouth , before it either got stolen or I swapped it for the fuckin watery cabbage I loved.

Then the clattering of the trays being thrown onto a service table after everyone finished at virtually the same time.

Very scary experience on your first day when you have just pissed the bed got away with it and started to settle down talking to inmates which are on my table.

A screw came in and started to roll call.

"Laundry" he would bellow out, then approx 10 inmates would stand up and go to a screw waiting near the canteen door.

"Orderlies" he would bellow out again, and then another 10 would stand up.

Gardening, farm, cleaners, kitchen, toilets, gym etc.

It went on until every lad was out of the dining room apart from 4-6 of us.

We were then grouped together on a table and a social worker type bloke took us away, patches on his elbows, (you know the type).

Not frog marched, just a casual walk to a classroom, but we did see a lot of frogmarching going on and knew we would have to do this pretty soon.

He told us about what is about to happen, he was concerned about our welfare and we could talk to him at any time, another blah blah blah talking to, he gave us suicide leaflets, educational leaflets, prison pamphlets, Gideon bible, rules of the prison, he made a reference that it would have been nice to be given a pontins booklet really but that wasn't happening, smug tweed wearing twat. (O.m.g is that now racist, am I allowed to say that?).

(he later became our school teacher , educational officer , queue orderly at tea time , our guardian angel when playing extreme sports on the field and in the morgue (I mean basket ball court) and he wore the longest of dangliest of key chains , the new age hippy really wanted to be a screw)

I would love to mention his name but alas I cannot so I will refer to him as Graham.

Graham took us back to the canteen area to be met by another screw, he took us to the head warden, and (governor) stand to attention whilst being spoken to would be his words to the 4-6 of us when in the governor's room.

wasn't crying but the lad next to me was.

This was just a small lecture on what was expected of us whilst in his care, not once did he call us by our names just referred to us as a number.

My number was TF496254 Draycott Sir; this you could shorten to the last three numbers so 254 Draycott sirs.

Then it was off to get allocated jobs , I was sent to Mr xxxxx , one ugly wanker , round face who thought he was the bollocks , army tattoos up his arms , not that well done either .

He was the cleaning screw for that week; I think he hated it as he was constantly shouting at us.

Now how do I describe what I did for the first month on that floor?

We are given each either a mop , a scrubber , a big long bar of soap (stunk to high heaven , carbolic I think the name is , another thing I suppose I will have to research , is this book ever going to end ?)

But the one thing no one wanted was the buffers , this was like a curling stone (but rectangle) on a 6ft broom stick , they were heavy , oh my was they were heavy .

This you had to pull back and forwards on the floor, this is after the moppers have gone along first then the lad who carries the long bar of soap to get rid of the rubber scuffs left by the screws shoes, they scuffed it on purpose, Mr Brown was constantly scraping the side of his shoe on the floor, yelling for the inmate to get back and scrub it off.

The buffering was done by 1 inmate for approx 2-3 hours on the M1, back and forwards , back and forwards , aggghhhh , if you finished it early you would go back and start again until near on lunch time , then after lunch it would be the corridor cell legs coming off the M1 .

That floor would be shining for the dinner time march to the canteen, if the buffer did not buff we placed an old jumper underneath it to polish better.

We had rest bite for around 1 hour after lunch to stay in our cells, tidy up and do things like nothing really, I had no pictures, no books, and no nothing for a few days when the book trolley inmate would come around and give us 1 minute to choose 2 books.

The first few nights would be very lonely indeed , even though I hid my bed wetting on the first night , I got sussed out when it was laundry day and I had a massive round orange patch on my sheet and the room did smell a little .

They inspect the sheets when you placed them in the laundry basket (oooh the laundry basket?) just in case you have ripped some off to make rope swings to other inmates or you have decided to strangle yourself.

I was given extra chores for this bed wetting, one chore that everyone knew you did something bad was to polish the captains bell in the corridor, not just a little wipe but a full on shine with brasso, it took ages and then you did it again, the shiniest thing I had ever seen, big plated rope hanging down from the bell, it was impressive.

Day 2 or 3 – gym.

This gym was like no other, I don't think I will be able to describe this gym in little words so please bear with me and read this page again if it does not sense, it makes sense to me.

The gym was a little bigger than basket ball court, set up in the morning by inmates was a circuit training course around the circumference of the hall, above each obstacle was a plaque with 3 colours on it red, green, & black and next to that colour would be number, this number corresponded to how many times you had to do that obstacle,

So if it was push ups, green x10, red x 20, black x 30

Medicine ball pick up green 15, red 30, black 45 etc.

Approx 20 obstacles to complete, so

The new inmates did the green, if you did something bad you would go onto red, if you came back again to detention centre you would go onto black.

This was a killer, every inmate would tire out half way around, I was no exception, I was knackered, if you gave up through exhaustion half way around they would put you on red to finish the course, it did not matter how long it took you, you had to do it and I have missed out on recreation time due to me being short and fat.

The hardest I think was the pull up bars and the bench lift, one end of a bench would be placed on the wall and you had to lift it 20 times from the other end, squat thrusting as you did it, they placed this half way around and it would virtually kill you off, collapse is an understatement.

I am not going to say much about the second visit here later so while I'm her I will tell you on my second visit I did the black course and inmates were looking at me in awe of how easy I was completing this, this tells you the first time it worked, second time around I was built like a brick shit house 5.8 tall compared to my 4ft nothing I was at this time.

The cabbage , that's what did it , (but I think was in D.C , 2nd time) I think at every lunch time we had watery cabbage and I loved it , loads of salt , I would eat others who left it or swap my dried mash potatoes (they didn't stick milk , egg , mayo or even a pinch of black Mediterranean sea salt in it . (I had to look up how to spell mediteranian)

Lunch time at 1pm was small and mainly a cheap chicken burger, scrambled eggs, spaghetti, mash, treated at the weekend to steak Dianne though.

Tea time at 5pm would be a bit more substantial but on the same lines as lunch I think, but to tell you the truth I cannot really remember tea time to much?

We would work at prospective jobs until tea time , some inmates who have earnt it would go into the recreational room to either play pool or watch some crap on TV , the TV being 8ft up on the wall so no one could change channels and a grill , mesh over the front so you could not smash it ? .

Pool table was tea stained with balls missing , 1 cue , a card table , chess etc I think I went in the rec room a couple of times , I preferred to read in my cell .

After a week we were allocated different jobs which we would stay in during our vacation.

Mine was laundry as I kept my nose clean the first month , I was liked by the screws , I was the one who would just do his time , get on with it , leave and realise his mistakes and not to return , HA .

Every week on the first visit regardless of whether we would be out on the rugby field, on both occasions not once did I play football, the rugby was just one massive scrum, fighting, kicking, punching and gonad grabbing it all happened here.

It hurt a lot , encouraged by the screws to get stuck in , I was the soft one so I got the kicking most of the time , 1 screw kicking me back onto the pitch when I limped off , I limped on the pitch in a worse condition .

On par with this was the medicine ball chase in the sports hall, a group of 100 would be separated into 2 groups, a medicine ball in the middle of the hall barely big enough for the inmates.

The ball had to get to the oppositions side of the room to touch the wall, 40-50 of us racing towards that ball to get it first, you really did not want to be first and I never was, I was wise.

The brawl was worse than a Spanish street bull chase, blood, broken ribs, fingers or toes.

I did see it on a few occasions inmates being carried out, oh what fun.

My laundry detail was to collect sheets, give out sheets and generally do the laundry with 4 others, large ironing machines, massive washing machines and driers.

I obviously had the best clothes, the best ironed, and in some sense designer as my shirts were granddad collar, not allowed but never questioned.

I sold new towels for mars bars or sugar, new jeans for double that and so much more.

My cell by month 2 was infested with toothpaste, sweets, oh virtually anything you could get at the tuc shop.

Wages where approx £0.80-£2.20 per week but considering you could buy a mars bar for 8p-ish that was ok wages for then.

On my second visit I was an orderly in the clothes exchange programme so in the laundry many times , I also had to change the towels in the screws mini kitchen every day and every day I stole the fag butts from the ashtrays in the mess , I would sell these fag butts , half a match and some strike for approx 3 mars bars worth of chocolate , I did not smoke but I sold so many that I was No 1 salesman on the wing , passing them to library man to pass on to the inmate and he would bring me back my goodies .

I was grassed on by a lad who worked in the laundry, a little Indian lad told the screws that I was taking fag butts and selling them, oh the shit hit the fan then.

I went mad with him after I came back from the governor's office; I was placed on punishment for 2 days.

This means I had to do red circuit training in the morning and in the afternoon for 2 days, then back to the laundry.

My day back at the laundry I questioned why he would do this, little fuckin grass, I fuckin hated a grass, (and still do)

After a slight misunderstanding I pushed him in the wicker laundry basket 4ft x3ft x4ft deep.

Big leather straps held the top to the basket, he went in backwards, and I did up the straps, job done.

I carried on with my day up until 4.30pm when we finished, by then he was in the basket for approx 1 hour in the back store room.

We were all back in our cells when the screw came around for the roll call before tea time.

2 mins later the alarms started to ring , double lock down (this is when they drop the handle on the door , close your door window flaps etc , they then do a room searched just in case the absconder is hiding , a very quick response .

I'm not too sure but I think it was around 8-10pm when my door opened.

"Draycott 254 sir "I yelled as I stood up

2 burley screws came into the room , 1 turned to face the corridor in the doorway , the screw in front of me drew back his hand , (I thought to tap the other screw on the shoulder or something)he then gave me the biggest and heaviest of slaps on my face , right across the cheek and making me fall back on the bed (am I allowed to mention a name ?), that hurt , that hurt a lot , I obviously cried as that's what I did ,they stood there looking at me until I composed myself and took me to the governor .

 "254 Draycott sir".

" 254 Draycott " he said , sorry I forgot most of what he talked about as he was screaming and talking quietly at me , he was the good cop bad cop in one , basically I lost 2 weeks , this means that I was to stay in Eastwood park for another 2 weeks on top of my sentence , he told me this was the biggest security alert they have had in the history of Eastwood park and I was a disgrace , considering it had only opened a couple of years before it wasn't that bad .

They heard him screaming at 7pm that would have been 3 hours in the laundry basket.

Hell followed.

My circuit training was increased to black , no privileges , scrubbing the bell after it had already been done , last in the queue for breakfast , dinner and tea , all my new excess clothes , clean new laundry taken .

I was back to basics, the very basics you get when you walk through the door for the first time.

I got into a strict regime of training for nothing in particular, I just wanted to train and train again, and this was the second time around in D.C. I know for sure as the first time in DC I was fighting with a lad who talked like a yokel, that was over a bag of sugar (I lost a day remission for that but I can hardly remember it (so I can't put it), but this is when I was a bit stronger and tougher and was admired by other inmates for my strength of getting around a circuit in record time.

I would go train whilst others went to rec, I would buff that floor faster than anyone and do a brilliant job, Mr xxxx who slapped me had his boots polished daily by me, he would stand there on the M1 corridor whilst I polished his boots, he would then scuff the one boot with the other so I had to do it again, twat.

That last month was hell for me but I was respected by many to what I had done as still quite a bit of racism in the D.C. at that time.

31/03/82 Social report

Visit to timothy at Eastwood park dc , seemed quite pleased to see me as he said he didn't get any visitors , he spent a considerable amount of time telling me about how the centre operated , he had found the first few days filled with circuit training was the typical regime of how the centre was run .

His attitude towards the offences he had committed was very flippant + he said that he got a really good kick out of driving cars , he said he would probably continue when he was released , he said if he met up with tony like he did last time he would do the same again .

The next few inserts from social reports have been blanked out due to names being mentioned.

In these following file pages attached to the reports from above my mother questions the social services on whether she can visit and get money from the office for bus fare on 3 occasions and if they would supply fresh clothes when I leave (*aggh bless her*) ,

Social services have blanked off a very lot in the next 4 pages of my reports so troubles must have been had at home , mum was going out with a ruffian , dad was going out with a lady who was in turmoil with my mother , wow would they bitch , I ended up really liking this lady , she moved into my granddads house in Castlefields with my father , I think my mother was really bitter about this as she was a lovely lady we talked virtually every month for the past 20 years *(she passed away earlier this year 2020)*.

16/04/1982 social report

Office visit by Mrs Draycott, she wanted to visit timothy but I pointed out that he would be released 23-4-82 , she asked if she could go down with me to pick her son up but I informed her I would be on holiday , I said I would ask Mr Carson if she could accompany her .

The rest is blanked off apart from a report from Eastwood Park to Mrs Waring my social worker.

7/4/81 - summary Eastwood park social services to Shrewsbury social services. (All hand written)

Timothy (10/3/67) has been in the care system since June 1980 following more criminal offences and court appearances , timothy is the youngest of a well known family in his home town (how the fuck would you know that ?).

Timothy is a likable lad and has got away with a lot through his pleasant nature in the past and we feel he is intent on a criminal career.

Now in Eastwood Park he seems at time very childish and his attitude towards the system is none caring.

Through conversations with timothy we understand he will be returning to St Gilberts School to complete his care order.

Progress poor but considerable social work involvement very likely to be required.

This was my closing report from the warden (first visit)

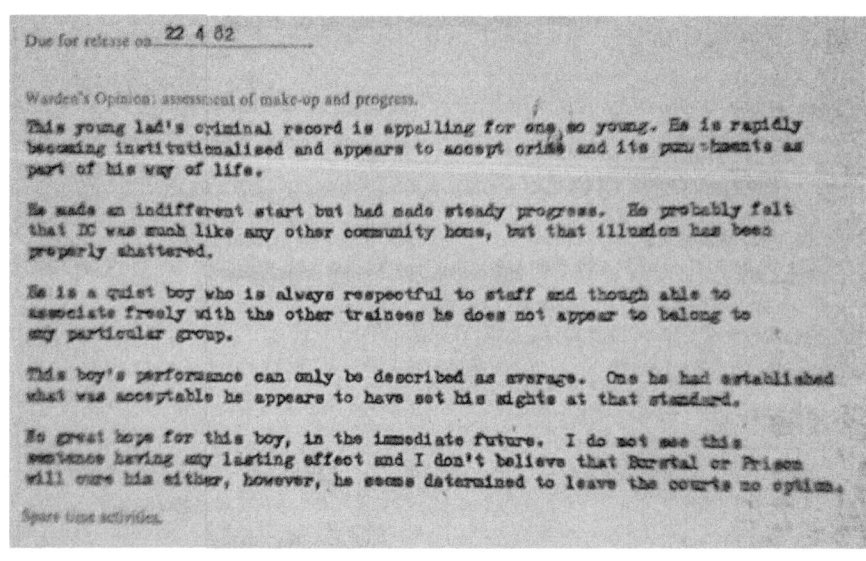

Due for release on __22 4 82__

Warden's Opinion: assessment of make-up and progress.

This young lad's criminal record is appalling for one so young. He is rapidly becoming institutionalised and appears to accept crime and its punishments as part of his way of life.

He made an indifferent start but had made steady progress. He probably felt that IC was much like any other community home, but that illusion has been properly shattered.

He is a quiet boy who is always respectful to staff and though able to associate freely with the other trainees he does not appear to belong to any particular group.

This boy's performance can only be described as average. Once he had established what was acceptable he appears to have set his sights at that standard.

No great hope for this boy, in the immediate future. I do not see this sentence having any lasting effect and I don't believe that Borstal or Prison will cure him either, however, he seems determined to leave the courts no option.

Spare time activities

Well what can I say , I think everyone had it in for me , I mean I was a likable lad with a cheeky smile that would melt your heart and you know them cute puppy eyes that look up at you begging   , yep , that was me .

He should not have said Borstal in that last sentence as it got abolished by then, naughty warden.

As Mentioned I don't remember too much about which visit as it was mainly all the same routine but things I do remember apart from what I have written about.

Being kicked heavily by a screw on the rugby field (I know his name)

Having my ear pulled and being virtually dragged down the corridor, enough for me to be doubled over.

Being slapped numerous times across the head, having my fingers pulled back by the screws, toes being stamped on so your shoes or boots are not clean, enabling them to give you extra punishment.

I was delegated to pick up the shit parcels from outside the cell windows as not a lot of lads wanted to shit in the potty so they shit in a paper and make a parcel out of it , hence shit parcel , I did a shit parcel on a couple of occasions (not when I was picking them up though).

When on this duty I often picked up items which the lads had accidently thrown on the ground when attempting to rope swing items to next doors cell, on one occasion I found some whole ciggies tied up with string, now how the fuck did they get them and where did they get them, didn't matter really as I sold them Sport on the second occasion was for me if it involved any sport I would get involved (apart from rugby, basket ball was my forte.

The second time around I was not a liked lad by the main screws due to what I had done (they all remembered me and I really do mean all of them) , I got one over them and it was not intentional , more of an accident that I did up the straps to the laundry basket .

But I do remember the good time also, I remember only cleaning the toilets once on this particular day, I was chuffed, very very happy, enough to go to the rec room and socialize and where I found Brian who I had stolen loads of cars with in Shrewsbury sitting in the room alone in front of the TV, apparently he had been there for a few days, he saw my name on the roll call board but was too scared to come down that corridor.

I gave him all my things I did not take (posters , books , toothpaste , what I had really) and off I went on my jolly

Fuck me I was due for release the next day, that poor fucker.

I remember the second visit on the medicine ball football , I kicked fuck out of loads , I didn't give a shit , I ended up loving it , as did I the circuit training .

Without D.C I would not be who I am now (that doesn't make sense so I will probably come back to that , unless my proof reader notices it) err , I don't have a proof reader .

Everyone is telling me about spell checker but it hasn't flagged up any red yet so I will carry on writing until my keys are <u>unseeable</u>.

Wow...Day of release, 254 Draycott sir "your going to be back Draycott, and it won't be to long either ", the reception screw said.

That was nice of him to say, full of optimism for my future he was.

I gathered up my measly belongings and probable 1980s tank top, I also probably looked a right pleb.

Mr Mackie, the governor did not see me off

Actually they were right, I think it was 3 months later but I will come to that later.

This is the probation officers report on my first few days in D.C, not the social workers (so confusing sometimes)

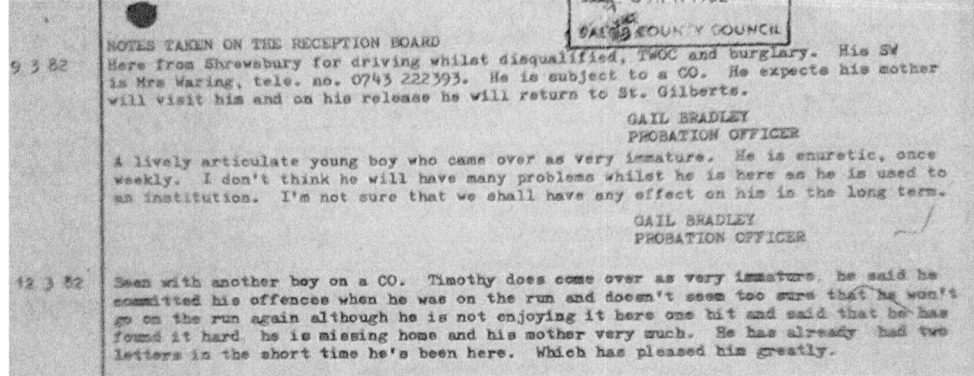

I got to see how remote this place was and what I didn't get to see out of my window every day , which was not a lot really as my cell window was facing a brick wall with a small patch of grass outside , the other times was on the rugby pitch surrounded by a barb wire topped fence at least 30ft tall , surrounded by trees .

On both occasions I didn't get to go out much as being laundry and mess orderly you are mainly inside the complex.

I was due to be picked up by a social worker and taken back to St Gilberts, No mother to accompany the social worker; she did promise in the letters that she would come.

I do not remember being picked up or the journey back – memory blank time

By the reading of my report I was not to down hearted on the journey back , Mr Carson does not write to well so I have done my best in deciphering , some bits are missing that I wish I could understand . 23/4/82 (Mr Carson? probably another elbow patch social worker)

"Collected timothy from Eastwood Park, he was very pleased to be out but could give no assurances that he would not get in trouble again if tony turned up.

Timothy seemed happy to get back to St Gilberts saying he felt like his was home , he directed me from the motorway to the door (ha I was the 1980s version of sat nav) .

At St Gilberts Timothy's friends showed me around the school & Tim became increasingly appreciative of St Gilberts, I said he would much prefer to be here than D.C. , he said he would try to keep out of trouble , however he said he would feel obliged to go if someone like tony contacted him or turned up , due to loyalty , he could not be distracted from this thought , which did not bode to well .

28-4-81 (Mrs waring back from holiday)

Collected timothy From St Gilberts to take him to Wrekin Juvenile court, two year conditional discharge, returned him to St Gilberts.

 Wait a min, read it yourself, my fingers are getting tired and I need a cup of tea.

I'm not even going to bother reading it myself so hopefully nothing bad.

Ok I had a peep

So to sum up so far , 1.5ft taller , fit as fuck with knowledge of how to steal the new shape fords (sierras , escorts) how to hot wire VW cars with ease , and weirdly I really think I came out better looking .

1 week Back at St Gilberts, I think this will be chapter 4 or 5, I'm not too sure.

Well, this does not read well, I thought I had grown up and sort of turned over a new leaf.

St Gilberts report within a month of returning, read this, it made me laugh.

This is after the first time around at the detention centre.

This is Tim's second review since he has been at St.Gilberts. He presents as a very likeable boy but this tends to be only artificial. Tim was the first boy to go straight from a basic card onto a weekly card but in January this year he was put onto a daily card because of his abscondings and the offences committed while he was on the run. Tim was sent to Detention Centre in March and it seems very sad that since his return to St.Gilberts he has once again not yet earned his weekly card.

Tim's relationships with adults seem to be very superficial. He also tends to be very attention seeking, this usually takes the form of his being very childish and immature. He relates well to one member of staff but this basically is only to try and get his own way.

Within the peer group Tim is an outsider. He has not made a real friendship with any boy. The more mature boys in the group tend to leave him alone because of his very childish, immature and often babyish attitude and behaviour. This means that Tim tends to gravitate towards the other 'idiots' in the group which often leads him into trouble.

Tim's home contact has now once again become regular. He goes home for weekend leave and long holidays and now always returns on time and speaks highly of home and that he has enjoyed himself.

Mrs Waring (*Jacquie* to her friends, notice how she changes her date system – as written in the file, I found it weird or have I got OCD?).

May 8th – 1982 – *Home leave for the weekend at mothers?*

May 25th – 1982 *visit to see if Tim could go home for 10 days half term to his fathers, Mr Draycott agreed to this at new park close.*

May 28th *took Tim to his dad's house for 10 days home leave.*

3/6/82 visit to Tim at his dads house , everything going well , Mr Draycott allowed Tim to camp out a couple of nights.

7.6.81 Telephone call from Timothy to say that he had had a tiff with his father about a radio that had gone missing and he couldn't get back into the house for his CSE files , suggested to Tim to get himself back to school as planned and I would try to arrange to get the file back.

8.6.81 t/c to Mr Draycott, spoke to his girlfriend, she said Tim had called back later to collect the file but his father was very angry with him over this radio, I arranged to call the following evening.

9/6/81, spoke to Tim's fathers girlfriend who told me she would not think it would be possible to come back for weekend leaves at new park close but we agreed that his father would contact St Gilberts to arrange something.

10.6.81 t/c call to St Gilberts to pass on this

20/6/81, Tim has gone to school camp.

Sometime in July 1982.

Maggie was in full flow of being our prime minister and I was 15, not political at all, I think the Falkland's conflict made everyone political but a friend of mine got really narked when the Government decided to sell of half the shares of British telecom (our adorable buzby bird soon to leave us).

The miners' strike was around this time and every friend's dad seemed to be involved in that, Arthur Scargill was such a funny looking man every time he was on the news, always very shouty, I was too young and rebellious to give a shit

We were singing Willie Whitelaw's willy at this time , which was a punk record and very easily remembered , look it up , you will like it ,and if you're wondering who willy Whitelaw is look that up as well .

Dave a friend of mine and 2 years older than me, a punk who was very political, so whilst on an absconding trip we hooked up, got drunk and started to cause trouble.

This one I did not get caught for I think mainly because I was drunk was the police station funny night out trip.

Myself and the above mentioned gathered up loads and loads of for sale signs from the Monkmoor area , a newish housing estate around the Conway drive area was being built at the time so that was an ideal place to gather them up , we made countless journeys and not once at 1-3am in the morning whilst drunk did the police come out of the station , we placed in excess of 50-70 for sale signs (banged in the ground) in front of the cop shop on the lawn , very very funny to look at

Never heard about it again? , I often wonder if any houses got sold in that Conway drive area in that year, mmm baffling I think I will study that one.

But basically that was Dave's political statement about Maggie Thatcher selling everything off. (I don't think I will be mentioning in this book about me and Maggie Thatcher at the inauguration of the channel tunnel , I might get sued).

As mentioned I had 3 months away from detention centre back at St Gilberts , in this 3 months I kept up my training and getting in the squash court down the back of the home , I'm trying to think hard but I am sure it was in the middle of a field , a standalone building down a little track to the middle of the farmers field , it had the tiniest of rooms in the foyer , no room to change , basically straight into the squash court , it was also used by the locals and on a few occasions I had to relinquish my place for the adults .

We filled in a book when we wanted to book the court; I had that court at least 5 times a week for a few hours a week (More when I came out of D.C for the second time)

Blue spotted ball , perfect weight for me to train with but played a red or yellow spotted ball whilst playing with the housemasters and the Hartlebury neighbours , fuck me did I whip some ass in the squash court when I was a 15 year old fat kid.

Slazenger power play something was my fav , round head , my teacher had the new fibre glass racket , mine was a hand me down from Mal a care worker who taught me mainly .

I must have got through at least 5 rackets in my time in that court and I distinctly remember robbing the sports shop in Telford and gathered many a squash racket (court charge sheet below)

This squash court was my sanctum, my retreat, my getaway from what was happening in that house.

(Within these 3 months in between Detention centres).

I will get straight in with this and I do not want to write about or linger my mind on it too much.

Orphan lad (cannot name or describe him)aged 12/13 mental age of a 9 yr old, mentally handicapped lad I witnessed being abused by a house master (we will call him Mr C as we are up to that in the alphabet), as usual with me accidently walked in on them and stood there shocked , I could go into detail about this but I really cannot , this same abuser tried it with me many times which I will tell you about very shortly .

Junior a very good friend who took the piss out of me when I arrived but soon become a friend decided to pick on me to join him in the attic space (you didn't say no to Junior).

We climbed the thin corridor walls like spider men until we got to the hatch in the middle of the ceiling , held our legs akimbo as we climbed through , height approx 30ft room floor to ceiling space , free climbing up an alley way wall , amazing .

The attic space above our bedroom was vast, nothing in it all apart from rafters and wattle and dorb ceiling roof.

Junior got the evostick glue out and proceeded to put it in a little cellophane bag, he started to suck on the bag and then exhale, I think I was looking on in awe at what he was doing.

I had never done drugs before apart from the odd drag of a fag , was I really going to participate in this when I have said no to loads by then .

"Give me that" he didn't give it me, greedy fucker had another suck then another.

I really wanted some and got my chance when his head started to dip and the massive grin appeared (his grin was truly amazing).

I took the bag and copied what he had done, in, out, in, out

Well as you can imagine I cannot remember to much of what I was thinking apart from laughing , my head was spinning but I didn't care about that , in fact I didn't care about anything , anything at all ,not even the 20,000 brain cells I had just destroyed.

Junior stood up and suddenly went crashing through the middle of the joists , leg dangling in midair through the ceiling into our room below , plaster , wood and horse hair everywhere .

More laughter.

Junior decided to free fall onto a bed, made it and didn't make it; I was out of my face looking down on him and what I can remember still laughing.

But it didn't take long for me to realise what had happened and I was at the hatch, clambering crab wise down the corridor walls.

I didn't tell a house master , I ran away , there and then , Paul from Willinhall trying to stop me as I was gathering up stuff out of my face

29/07/82 court

Taking a vehicle without authority, taking a conveyance without authority, Burglary, theft from a vehicle,

I left St Gilberts when it was getting dark and as always proceeded along the fields.

Now I know this sounds corny due to what I was going through in my head , but a delivery van with a mushroom logo was at a farm with the keys in it , bonus . (I was sober by then I'm sure)

But this would be the van I stole to get away from the drugs whilst it was still circulating in my brain.

This van got me all the way back from Hartlebury to Shrewsbury, I stayed in a cardboard box under the station bridge for a few days with mates looking after me, never the air raid shelter again after being grassed upon and more people knew about it now, I broke into the cycle shop in abbey Foregate and managed to get a bit of money to get further away, they would sure to find me in my own town.

I had a feeling I could stay away as I had done a bit of survival training , I knew the basics and I was confident I could kill an animal after the farm training I had been through .

I met up with Tony some place? And we proceeded to hitchhike to get out of town or to get a car en-route to apologise to my blonde haired ex girlfriend in Machynlleth.

We got picked up before we left the boundary of the town , nice couple who said they were going to mid Wales , we told them we had missed our bus to the Machynlleth as we were meeting a group , tony looked and was old enough to hitch , and it was rife then , no way can you do that now .

They gave us a lift to Welshpool little railway , we hitched again by a bloke in a jag , he took us to Machynlleth , nervous as wickety wick wick gobblygook we went down the lane to the farm , we were going to pay our pitch fee to the mother or father and sleep a couple of nights and carry on .

She came to the door when we rang at first did not recognise me, did the usual thing of sticking a finger up and pondering "where have I seen this boy before ".

We paid for the weekend and made camp, giving some excuse about why we were camping alone.

Morning came along; we got up, stole a car from a farm a few miles away and headed back to Shrewsbury.

28/7/82 – Social services.

Received a phone call from Shrewsbury police saying they have Timothy and another boy in custody over a few mothering offences .agreed to attend the meeting.

Visit to the station, both boys admitted to the thefts but would not say anything in interview.

Spoke to the police and they have said that timothy will attend a special court in the morning , phoned Mrs Draycott and she seemed less concerned about Timothy as she has her Boyfriend around at the moment , she said she might come to court but as she was short of money she had to feed her boyfriends Dogs .

Excerpts from social enquiry reports 29.7.82, for Shrewsbury Juvenile.

These are the conclusions from social enquiry reports, it does go on for around 6 X A4 pages, but I've just spent 6 months telling you what they have just said.

So conclusion for the magistrates typed by my social worker, Mrs. waring –lovely lady.

Timothy Wayne DRAYCOTT continued/......

CONCLUSIONS AND RECOMMENDATIONS :

Throughout his life Timothy has been exposed to a considerable degree of instability and insecurity in his home background. During his early adolescence he consistently presented as childish and immature and has committed an alarming number of offences for one so young. To date he has been dealt with by a variety of custodial and non-custodial methods culminating in a second period of detention in August 1982.

Since his return to school following detention Timothy has made considerable efforts to improve his behaviour and attitude within the school and has shown increasing signs of maturity. He has not absconded from the school since July 1982 although this was initially a major problem with Timothy.

Unfortunately, through a renewed association with his co-offender Anthony Dodd, Tim's behaviour outside of school has been less satisfactory in recent weeks. Some of the responsibility for this would seem to lie in the lack of supervision available to Timothy while on home leave, but the ultimate responsibility for offending is Timothy's. Timothy must accept this and learn to utilise the maturity and self control he is able to demonstrate within the school setting in his actions outside the school. It is hoped that the further twelve months offered by the school would enable him to do this more effectively as well as to increase and develop his independance.

The court may well feel that in view of Timothy's appalling record of offending and the thoughtless manner in which these present offences occurred at a period when Tim was making such good progress at school, that the time has come to consider a longer period of custodial treatment for Timothy.

Under the recent Criminal Justice Act Timothy could be liable to a maximum of twelve months Youth Custody if the court felt that such an order were essential for the protection of the public, or that the offences were too serious to justify a non-custodial sentence or that Timothy would not respond to such an alternative.

We would argue that the first two criteria are not met in Timothy's case bearing in mind that as far as the motoring offences are concerned Timothy is probably not the prime mover either in gaining entry to the vehicles or certainly in driving them even though he is no doubt a willing accomplice.

On the third criteria we would respectfully suggest to your Worships that there is a reasonable non-custodial alternative in Timothy's case in the form of the new residential Care Order. Timothy is already subject to a Care Order under Section 7 of the 1969 Children and Young Persons Act and so would be eligible on that basis for consideration to be given to this type of sentence.

We have already outlined to your Worships our plans for Timothy's future over the next twelve months had these offences not occurred. It also seems apparent that the main area of concern with Timothy is his behaviour while he is not under the direct supervision of the local authority, particularly when he is on home leave. The imposition of a residential Care Order would therefore enable us to continue our long term programme with Timothy and at the same time considerably restrict the opportunities available to him for re-offending.

Continued/........

So back to court on these measly charges, when they said you're going down again to me, my tear ducts opened, I knew exactly what I was going to be doing their, the trouble I had been in before in Eastwood park, the black circuit training every day, I bawled and I bawled loudly, thing about it now it was embarrassing, stupid little immature child I was.

I did not want to leave that court as it was so unexpected, kids don't go down again for just stealing a few cars and robbing a bike shop and some other minor stuff, surely, this one did.

And they extended my care order to 18 years old, 3 months detention centre based on the report Mrs waring had done for me above.

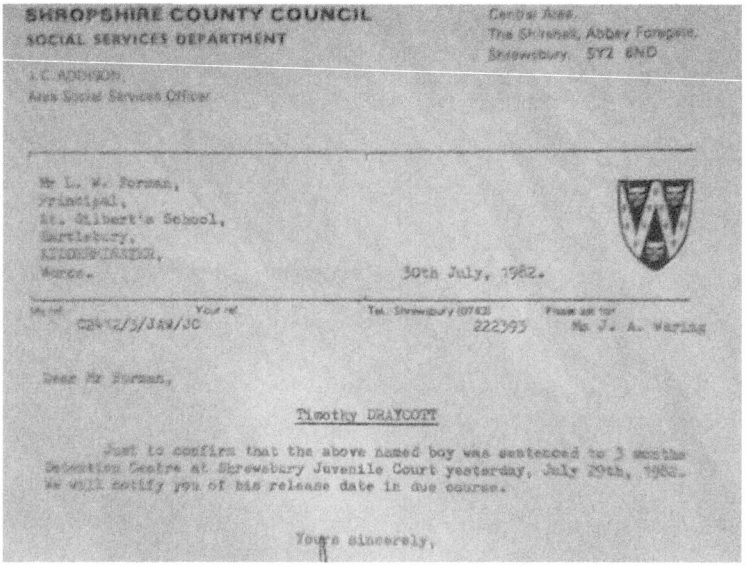

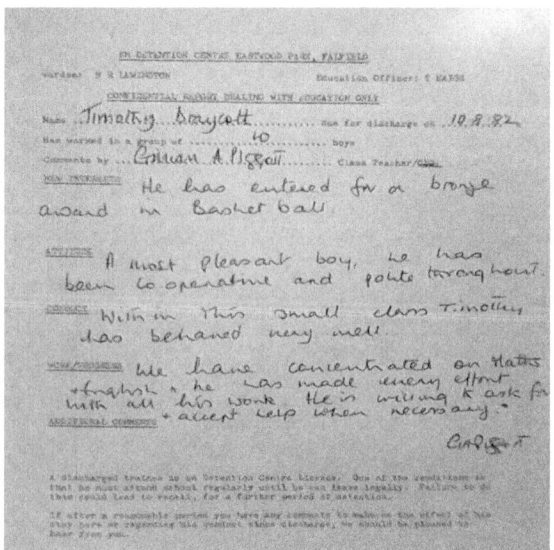

Release date, yeah, 10th September 1982.

So I did my second sentence , as mentioned I have combined them in previous pages as it was one of the long numb experience in my life .(*other numb bits in my life , my first love* when I was 20 who told social services she had never loved me , even thought she just gave birth to my first born , my beloved Amanda , my mother and my last girlfriend of 3 years , numb or not they all inspired me to finish this book).

Right the magnifying glass comes out again for the next files as its going to take me a while to try and decipher, I'm back from Cyprus and back in my flat in Shrewsbury.

This weekend I will be gallivanting around the country to get more info and to take photos.

I'm going to see a friend who I not seen in over 30 years from St Gilberts , I was surprised when I found him through social media , scared at first to contact him , but I did (and I did find another 3 lads on social media from various Homes but the conversation did not go far.

Chapter, the wet sports chapter.

So , where were we , it has been at least a month now since I have wrote anything so I have to go back a few chapters to see where I am .

It's been an interesting month in researching my book, so I am going to take time out and tell you what has occurred in this last month (apart from being in lockdown, but that didn't affect me as I was building at the time and builders had no restrictions –don't ask?.), I will keep it short and sweet as I know you would be eager to know what type of water sports I was involved in with the head teachers at St Gilberts.

So councils , file offices , newspapers have all closed down so I sent masses of emails to various places that could give me info , out of 5 Government departments 2 have replied , that was the police (ACRO) and Worcester County council saying all other info is privy .

I came from D.C for the second time I know I was a better person.

I was straight in the squash court, this training later got me into a local team, then a county team but I will come to that later.

We did a load of outward bound trips with St Gilberts; I did really love these trips.

I took my duke of Edinburgh award , what I did I do not know but I did a lot , climbed Snowden with Handicapped children when I was 16 but I will come to that also .

Whilst seeing a friend in the last month he has reminded me (amongst other things) about the Symonds yat rapids in Hereford.

We made canoes at St Gilberts and as soon as he said this I remembered the shed, the smell of the resin, the orange colour of the canoe, even down to what was hanging on the sheds walls, the waterfalls at Symonds yat, the canoeing at the farm in Machynlleth, the learning of barrel rolls in the river severn in the country in Worcestershire it all came flooding back to me, Amazing

Now I thought I remembered a lot but this lad was amazing I just needed to be reminded , he read through my St Gilberts paperwork and filled in many gaps in my life , it came flooding back and we had a cry at some point in the night but them tears soon cleared up , then a nice gin which I had took to give him , pissed , oh yeah , we drunk the bottle and more and had a great laugh , alas I cannot add him on social media as he wants to keep hidden (I don't blame him , this is hard , as I know I am going to get scrutinized)

I got into the water at Symonds yat , at a minibus stop off area , we all unloaded and got our spray decks , paddle etc and made our way down the bank , fairly high rapids at that time , they had obstacle courses down the river , I think they still do competition slalom .

The river at this point is surrounded by high trees, I have not been back since then so memory it is, the trees very dominating, top half of the rapids buildings like old mills or warehouses, that I remember.

I remember barrel rolling and getting a telling of as the others might copy me, *(when catering 25 years later I built a jetty for my then boss, he took me water skiing and I took to it on my first time, over the ramps and dipping low)*, so I was pretty good at water sports in my day, a sport I didn't take up as I was growing so fast I knew I would be in the basket ball team soon

Show off, fuck yes, I was up and down them rapids like a shot, I made moves that the staff would clap at, I was the only one to make it to the top of the rapids, *(that's that muscle I gained in D.C)*, that's all I can tell you about that as that's all I remember, just a bit of showing off and showboating by me, and why not I am a Pisces.

Right I'm eager to get this bit over and done with and I don't have to many words to express what I feel like every time I either tell anyone in my life about this or think about it and I think about it a lot, so it will either be a long sentence that I will type or I will stop a second and think of the words I have to say but either way it is from my memories that I can and will never forget.

We had a day trip to Kinver caves which is on the outskirts of Kidderminster , we had been a few times and its always a good place to visit (*they built houses in these caves in late 82 or 83 I think*) but the adventures we used to get up to at these caves , I was more interested in the writings and names on the walls and if I could find fossils or artefacts.

I do not know if this was planned or it was a accident but I seemed to be left behind , I was alone in my room when Mr C came in "what you doing here , didn't anyone tell you , everyone is at Kinver caves " , he offered to take me as he had to lock up the Kinver unit .

(Yeah I know, 30 miles apart Kinver unit at St Gilberts and Kinver caves – weird)

I didn't think twice about it , jumped in his car en-route to Kinver , he stopped in a lay by just outside Kidderminster , I questioned him and he told me (readers -you know what's coming don't you ?)that it had turned him on to see me watching him being sucked off, I told him about the other abusers I had met throughout my care days and I was not the one for him or anyone, he tried to talk me into it for a fair few minutes before I told him if he didn't drive I would tell on him, he drove to the caves, parked in the forest area car park.

"What makes you think that you deserve another chance in life, you have been given all the chances you will ever have "(or *something very similar*)

Now the abuser will know who he is when I post this book to him, as he said that to me a year later when I was taking my C.S.E's

He made a lunge for me, my seat belt was on, he held that in place while his other arm circled me and he started to kiss my neck, really slobbery.

Fuckin gross, I was clambering at the door handle to his (oooh nearly typed out the car make then that would have been libel?) car, he was pulling the door back in whilst still holding the belt socket but still over me, I cannot describe what he looked like or even the weight of the man but considering my size over his he was overpowering me, when he slammed the door shut he would grab and cupped my gonads, open the door again and he would shut it again so that's how it went for a few mins whilst he was still slobbering over me.

I mentioned again that I would say something if he did not let me out.

He let me out and I told a couple of lads , as usual we brush it off , have a laugh about it and carry on , I know they are more used to it than me as I was away for nearly 6 months in that year , I was being abused mentally in D.C .

So I'm going to get straight onto the second time with this perv, it did happen a year later but I'm going to roll this into one, I do not want to come back to this subject about his attempted abuse on me.

(Going forward a year, sometime in July 1984)Squash courts we booked out (me and Mr C) we met each other there as he was coming from home and I had a 100yrd walk.

Airplay we played and we played for at least an hour , which is pretty hard going but by this time I was a prolific squash and basket ball player , pretty fit in muscle (and looks) so I could keep up with any 30-40 yr old ,

I was thrashing (winning) the bloke until he nearly collapsed on me ,, elbows over my shoulders , holding me saying he was shattered and needed a hug , " fuck off Mr. C" , he didn't listen to me at all and embraced me then whilst holding his hands on my cheeks gave me a dirty kiss , holding my head against his trying to push his tongue in my mouth , I took a step back and swung my racquet in his face , one of his glasses on his rims shattered into his eye and I could (within seconds) see blood streaming down his face " are you ok " is all I think I said .

He was screaming , not with pain but the screaming of " please don't tell , I beg you , please , tell them it was an accident " , so I did tell them that it was accident at the house , he was a begging and whimpering cowered , like I was when I was being beaten by Mr A at Besford house 4 years earlier , whimpering piece of grovelling shit he is on that floor , I never experienced that before , that was new one on me , usually every time they are the force and we are the little chickens (did that make sense).

The trouble I have is , I know exactly where he works and it's not good , it's a place you would not like to see a pervert work (that statement dated Nov 2019), do I tell ? , no I don't think so , as I have mentioned at the very start , my word against theirs and a lengthy court hearing , which would cost me my remaining life .

Trouble is the bloody BBC also know this man as I told the reporters when they investigated St Gilberts from the 60s and 70s and came around to my house and took all the files (don't worry they signed a disclosure not to disclose my files but they brought them back totally muddled, (I can't help think I have told you that already though?).

But this is the Mr C who was being given head by a friend of mine , I think about this and how did he come to pressure that lad , same way he did with me , others , I just don't know , but I am glad I did not linger too much on that as it was a lot worse than I described , I am not one to glorify that behaviour , I don't even want to read back over it , I don't care about spelling mistakes or punctuation . (No I will not go back to it Mr Publisher).

We will come back to Mr C later during my work experience days at lo-cost food stores.

My friend who I visited knew about his antics (is antics to tame a word for this man?), but my friend was never approached by him but he was told by others what he was like, he also knew about the farm hand and one other housemaster that shocked me, really shocked me as I knew this housemaster and he was always nice to me (each to their own I suppose).

Right I can have a break after that and listen to Radio 6 iggy pop for a while , I am so glad I do not own a TV – poison .

I don't know when to start a new chapter and also I don't know what chapter we are on again so we shall call this Chapter 13, (the unlucky for some chapter).

I have just found this letter from myself to my social worker which I wrote in D.C 2/9/82.

I like how my writing style changes and interesting to know about me stealing my sisters moped, can't remember too much about it so cannot write about it, the bike was blue and it was a 50cc.

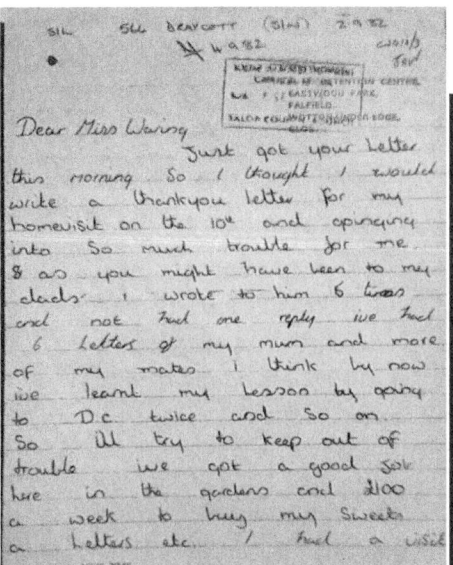

Going back a year now to the release from the second detention centre sentence .13/09/82.

As mentioned this was my wet sports, squash, basket ball year, let's carry on with my social enquiry reports, courts and criminal record to see what mischief I finished the year off with.

(Social report 13/9/82)

Tim Reported to me very punctual, very cheerful and in good spirits .Timothy had expected to go straight back to St Gilberts so had made the most of the weekend, he seemed quite positive about future family life but did admit that when he offends he enjoys it and can offer no guarantees that he would not do it again , he seemed quite confident about going back to St Gilberts and to slip back into the system , he has a geography field trip coming up next week for his c.s.e exam , It seems that St Gilberts expect him to stay until after the c.s.e exam results for June 83.

His earliest release would be his 16th Birthday , review set for 18/10/82 to allow Tim some time to settle back in (Mrs Draycott now back with her Boyfriend).

Quite a few reports hereafter I do not think I would bore you in things regarding my father saying I was a bad person and he does not see a future at his with his girlfriend and my sister staying weekends. (St Gilberts saying I am progressing in the month after my last D.C).

My Review was due soon which would decide if I stayed or left for my c.s.e.

First this is what I have to try to decipher and to read below that I was still wetting the bed

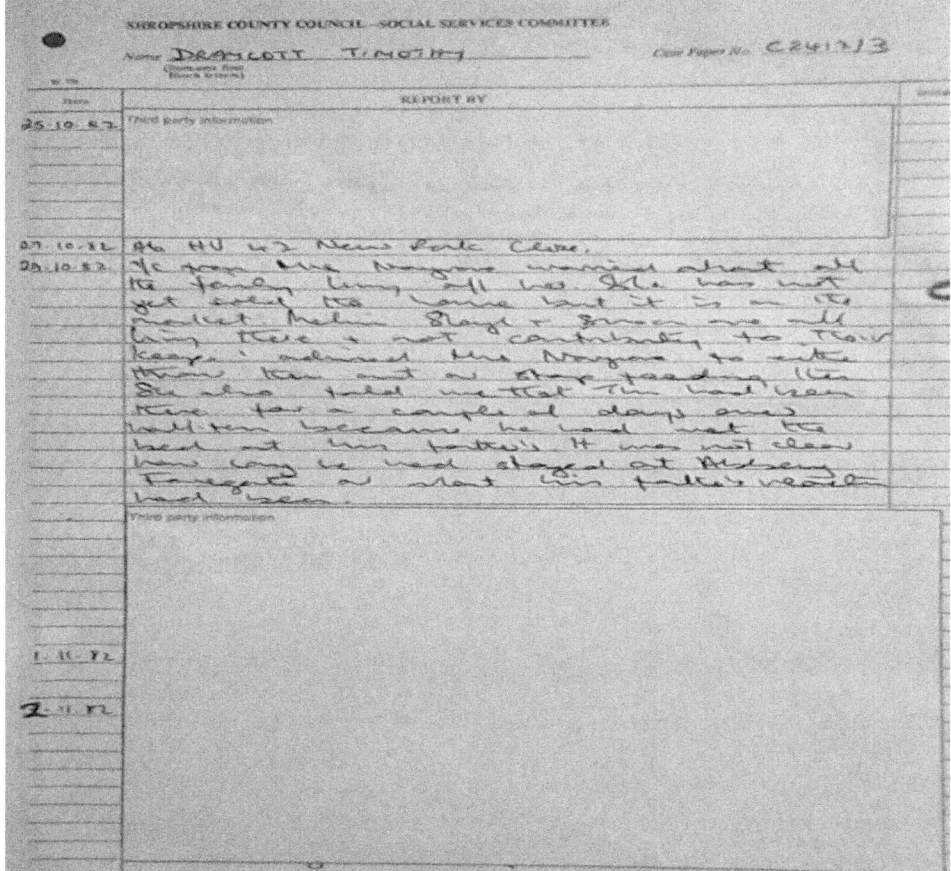

I do remember the many good times I had in late 1982 to early 1983 and if you do not mind I am going to share some of them memories with you, it's not all about the abuse and the car stealing.

I did some amazing tasks and projects (which I have studied intensely to place in my memoirs) that I am very proud of and think about very often , the fun times I had taking (amongst other activities)handicapped children up Snowden ---------------

The Duke of Edinburg awards set up in the late 1950s by the good ole queens husband to help take kids out of delinquent homes and give them a better life , 3 to 4 days camping doing orienteering , rummaging for mushrooms (ha , snuffling for truffles)and some team work , for that we got a lovely certificate (laminated), which I cannot find anywhere ? .

I was part of the youth of tomorrow apparently.

We set up camp in early October 1982 in a forest in Hereford, it was bloody freezing.

I did not need to attend this outward bound courses , they were mainly for the little uns for one but it was my half term holiday on the 21st October until the 1st November and I had been through this all before , but I did not refuse any visit out as I loved them (and still do

A group of around 10 of us went to this destination, if I knew where it was I would tell you but all my reports say that I was in Hereford learning outward bound skills, the only time I remember in Hereford is when we stayed in a private forest owned by the farmer who we beat the bushes for the pheasants to fly away and be shot.

(Later in life I catered for the mayoress in Shrewsbury when having my own catering company, she approached me and said "excuse me but are you the chef "

I was wearing chef's whites and a chef's hat at the time.

"Yes mayoress how may I help you" I politely followed with.

She then produced 2 lead shot from her hand and said she got them from the duck hoi sin and spring onion roll canapés I cooked and prepared.

"Oh Shit" I thought "I am so so sorry mayoress, I really did not see them, they should have been metal scanned ", I was bricking myself, the thought SUE came into mind.

"Oh no Chef, this is fantastic she said "it just goes to show that this is wild duck, you have made my day "

Shocked I was), so let's carry on; I thought that was little bit relevant at the time of writing.

Right I've put myself off, where was I, oh yeah.

We split into 3 groups with an adult in each group of 3 , we had to orienteer across the forest , around or up the hill and back to the forest camp site , first ones back had to put tea on , last ones back had to do washing up and pack down the following day .

Myself, Paul and another moved the mini flags from the hidden places to adjoining fences or trees without our house master seeing us, this really riled the housemaster who arrived second (2-3 hours after us and very dark), enough for him to slap my friend hard across the back, everyone cowered away apart from me, I confronted him and lashed out with a stick when he went to grab me.

I was then grabbed by a couple of lads as I think my temper got the better of me, the other housemaster still being out (probably lost in the wilderness).

It settled down when the one housemaster calmed the other down and I was sent to my tent , where I cried again , not in fear but this time in anger , I wanted to kill that basterd , always hated him and always will for what he tried to do to me he did to XXXX that day back at St Gilberts .

This anger streak would come back to haunt me on a couple of occasions until the age of 21 when I had my first child.

6790yyyyhhhyyyyyyyyhjyu – cat just walked over my keyboard. (It really did)

3.11.82   Social enquiry report sheet.

Visit to Timothys fathers house in New park close , saw Mr Draycott , apparently timothy had wet the bed on a couple of occasions when staying over the weekend , he tried to hide this by turning the mattress and putting the sheets in the wash , Mr Draycott had been surprised but not angry and was quite happy for Tim to return for any holidays , he is planning on getting a plastic sheet for the mattress so I agreed to get a proper one , his father has also said that he could get Tim a placement at a college that teaches thatching .

(A trade which my father's brother was in , his son is now a master Thatcher , I really should have taken that trade up , my father would have been proud of me .

A year later I would step through the doors of that college in Northampton and the following day I walked out and absconded – yet regret in life)

4.11.82 T/C to St Gilberts to advise them about a job situation , also explained the bed wetting over the weekend at his fathers , Tim has doubts about going to his father's again , they were surprised as Tim no longer does this at school , will have to keep an eye on this at its happening at home .

In-between these reports are a lot of blanked off pages they do not want me to know, but they go on for a few pages, it annoys me

18.11.82... *Seen Tim with his sister, they seemed in high spirits*

Yes, I know all that but I (and you) want to know about this blanked off writing.

I will go on the assumption that this is all to do with my mother and her then (new) boyfriend who was an angry man , he would lose his temper at the slightest thing , he hit my mother on a few occasions for looking at other men , my brothers warned him off and he calmed down , I'm not going to ask either of them but I am sure he got a belting from one of my brothers but I could be wrong as that definitely happened on the first boyfriend Richie when I was 12 and mother and biological father had separated .

15.12.82. *Home visit to Mr Draycott to advise Mr Draycott about Timothy's upcoming holiday, he had been notified and was expecting him the following evening.*

16.12.82 .*Telephone call to St Gilberts was informed timothy was in high spirits about his Christmas leave, he was looking forward to staying at his grans and fathers.*

30.12.82. *Home visit to Abbey Foregate saw Mrs Draycott , Timothys sister and Timothys grandmother Mrs Norgrove , the one brother has been evicted from his flat , Timothys other brother is pregnant , timothy it seems has been staying at abbey Foregate instead of his father's but Mrs Norgrove says he spends most of the nights out and does not return until the following morning , she has agreed to have timothy until the end of the holidays although everyone seemed vague about this , I felt there was more than 1 story that was being told.*

Timothy told me that he planned to go back to his father's for the weekend but his father's girlfriend was looking after her grandchild and his father was going to work over the New Year holiday.

5.1.83. *Mr Draycott says his girlfriend was still at his daughters but they may have split up, it has been on the cards for a while, he explained to me that Tim did not stay as much as he should and stayed out over night many times, at one time coming back at 1am covered in oil and smelling of petrol.*

7.1.83. *T/C to StGilberts Re Timothys w/e leave, explained the situation with the staff, I wanted to clarify where Tim would go for home breaks, arranged to ring back.*

Rang back , Timothy didn't want to speak to me at first but then said he didn't want to go home anymore , he said his father had told him to get lost and was adamant under any circumstances he would not go back , I asked Tim where he would like to go and he said to stay in a tent with a friend , I said this was totally unacceptable , he hung up .

Rang back and agreed with staff that Tim should stay at school this w/e; I would try to talk to him again on Monday.

10.1.83. *spoke to staff at St Gilberts and they said that Tim was still adamant that he did not want to go back to his fathers , Tim said he would go to his grans for the weekend as his mothers was too small .I said I would visit his grans to see if this was ok .*

13.1.83, *H/V to Abbey Foregate, Mrs Norgrove agreed to have Timothy over the weekends.*

Mrs Norgrove says she may be moving in the next couple of weeks to a house she has purchased in Cherry Orchard and it will have no room for timothy then.

H/V to New park close , Mr Draycott was adamant that timothy would not be staying at his house as he has problems of his own , I explained that timothy had know where to go and he said he can stay at his mothers , T/C To St Gilberts to explain that Timothy has know where to go .

Name: Tim Draycott

Case Paper No. _____

(Surname first
Block letters)

W.70

Date	REPORT BY	
17/1/83	Phone call from Mrs Musgrove confirming she is no longer able to cope with Tim & can not have him again at weekends	
20/1/83	Visit St Gilbert school. Saw care staff initially. Some problems with Tim & the w/e but now settled down & appears resigned to spending weekends at St Gilbert for the present. Later saw Tim who appeared pleased to see me & only to get out of the rep he was supposed to be doing at the time. He told me he could not go to his Nana any more & that he would not go to his Dads & rather would he go to his Mums as long as he was with Wilf. He said he was happy to remain at St Gilberts for weekends for the present.	
8.2.83	Hd to Mrs Draycott at 33 Tankerville St. She is happy to have Tim for weekends and has room for him even though the accommodation is cramped. She continued	
	third party information	
10.3.83	T/C from Sheryl to say that her mum was no longer living at 37 Tankerville St, having gone back to Wilf. She had apparently given Tony the keys to 37 and Sheryl thinks he is taking it over. Sheryl is now at her dads but it leaves Tim nothing though & any. Sheryl said that Mrs Draycott would have Tim now but it seems that Tim probably won't go. Also Mrs Musgrove is now in hospital. T/C to St Gilbert to advise them of the situation. Spoke to Tim who said he would like if his dads relatives happened. Agreed to try & sort out some alternative	

So basically my mother was gallivanting again around to her boyfriends and the rest of my family were all over the place – nothing new there then and just like my chapters are, so here is another – Chapter 20 something.

My grandmother could not cope with me so no going back there; she should have let me stay in that tent I suggested.

Visit to St Gilberts, they said they have been having problems with Tim's behaviour and tantrums that have been occurring but he seems to have settled down now the squash courts have been redecorated, Tim is happy that he is now in charge of the laundry cupboard (that funny), he is doing very well in his squash and has joined a local team, the main problem for Tim at the moment is a place to stay.

Tim has just taken his c.s.e and he thinks he has done very well in English , art and maths , Tim admitted that he started to cry for no reason when taking his geography and had to be excused , I asked about this and he said he started to think about his gran who was poorly .

I suggested to Tim we could try a residential place at a foster home locally to Shrewsbury but he was not interested in this idea , he said he would wait for his mother to be refocused and stay at St Gilberts in the meantime , he is staying the next two weekends as they have some activities they have on , we arranged to have a meeting to discuss Easter holidays and accommodation in or around Shropshire .

My reports for the next week or two go on to state that my mother could not be found, my grandmother was in hospital but had contacted St Gilberts to say that Timothy could stay at her new house in Portland view when she comes out of hospital, my social worker paid a visit to my aunties who was sympathetic towards me (aggh bless, I love my auntie Barb), I also wet the bed at St Gilberts a couple of times in the week.

Mum must be back at her Tankerville St property as she is welcome to have me back for the weekends (I'm sure will change very quickly ?) , and amongst other things Nan agreeing to having me over the Easter holidays .

The," oh let's not start this again" chapter.

5.4.83 social services report (Easter holidays)

Timothy came into the office today but I was busy with another client , I asked him to call back later but he did not come , called at Mrs Norgroves and she agreed to have Tim , at least he will have a roof over his head for the Easter holiday, I asked Mrs Norgrove to ring me if she thought it was too much for her , also left a message for Tim to call me .

7.4.83, No sign of Timothy

8.4.83, phoned police, Mrs Norgrove and visited Mrs Draycott, no one has heard from Timothy, I will call at Mr Draycotts. , 11.4.83, No sign of Timothy

13.4.83 Called in to see Mrs Norgrove, she said Timothy had called in, I asked if she get him to call me.

T/c from Shrewsbury police, Timothy has been arrested for 3 motoring offences.

I don't know why I relapsed on these , I was doing well at school , I was playing an abundance of sports , I was outward bounding and enjoying my life at St Gilberts , I wonder what went wrong .

I met up with Tony at the start of the holidays; he was now living with his girlfriend for a little while in Ditherington, Shrewsbury.

I crashed at his a few times ,it was a dump , the bath , kitchen floor , cups in fact everything was dirty , I may as well of said the only thing that was clean really , which was the water coming out of the tap ?(I would 3 years later get the next door flat , but tony had passed away by then) .

If it wasn't for the social worker telling me my crimes this one vehicle would have slipped me by as I thought the vehicle we actually used for the crime was taken from Shrewsbury.

Myself, tony and another friend broke into a place called teme-side self drive hire and took the keys to the brand new sierra 4x4, B plate, brand spanking new with less than a thousand miles on the clock a B plate blood red ford fiesta Mk2, I drove the little one as that is what I have always liked (even to this day at 6.4").

We got around £40 from the rental company office , Tony kept that money saying he can get beer later , I didn't drink and we had an argument about it , but it seems when I did eventually got back to St Gilberts I had money in my pocket .

Our friend left us when we got back to town in the cars, but he ended up grassing us up about the temeside car rental building, we drove around to get into more cars behind the lion hotel.

We ended up with loads of booty from cars which was all recovered when we had the police chase across the English bridge.

It all started with a police car was coming in the opposite direction when they saw the both of us , looking twice at me in the fiesta , that was it , I knew that they would turn around so I gunned it down to second gear and went flying past tony going up past the abbey church on a slight straight 30mph road , I was doing at least 70mph by the time I got to the traffic lights 1 mile from the bridge , I went straight through the red light , past my grandmothers old house and turned sharp left to my grans new house , no sign of tony .

I dumped the car a street away from my grans and went in the side alley, bedded down for the night and awoke to go find tony.

Totally amazed that he was in his flat, drunk in the morning, flat smelling of stale cider.

We went to see if his dumped car was in the 6 bells pub car park , wow it was so we jumped in and went to see if my fiesta was still in king street around 2 miles away .

It was but I cannot recall what Tonys answer was to the so called police chase past my grans house?

I do recall getting caught though and it's very memorable to me.

We drove around in Tony's stolen car as I did not want to drive in a car that may have been chased, we robbed the radio from it as that was a new style ford radio and they sold for a fiver.

We ran out of fuel near the golf course in Shrewsbury so we proceeded to a street called Kempsie Avenue , sneaking in amongst cars taking fuel for the sierra , Tony called me over to a car that had the keys in the ignition (to dark to tell what car it was) Tony jumped in told me to put the fuel in his stolen car and he will meet me at the old car scrap yard (Now a multiplex cinema) , I had a couple of glass bottles full so that should do it , I managed to get back to the posh car , unlocked the door with the keys tony gave me .

(You never can be too careful so always lock your car door and never ever place car or door keys on a hook by the front door , I have on a couple of occasions used a long stick to pull keys off a radiator by the front door and my arm through an open window to reach keys to cars)

I got in the car before putting the fuel in and as soon as I did get in the car a burly bloke banged into it , I straight away locked the door and reached over to lock the other not thinking about central locking on these new cars I think I opened up the doors again as on the passenger side another bloke went for my arm , I did what was natural to me and lashed out , he tripped back into the grass over the path , the other bloke had the driver's door open and was pulling my leg screaming at me to tell him where his car was .

The culprits to Tony's car had only gone and followed me back to this car.

I kicked out at the burly bloke and he also went back, I think stunned that a child of my age would do such a thing.

The doors were shut and it was catch 22, I could not move, I had 2 blokes either side of the car and soon to be 2 cop cars flashing lights behind me, game over when they found the radio to the fiesta but they never found tony, he did not know that I had been caught in his bloody car and I didn't get chance to drive it – gutted.

In police interview, social worker.

Tim was unusually subdued during interview and he broke down crying a few times , the police (d.c Roach)were surprised at this as they usually see Tim as quite a handful and non cooperative, they questioned him over the temeside van rental burglary which he denied and more offences from the previous weeks , D.C Roach says that if Tim admits these crimes they would not charge on the others , Tim Denied all charges , then admitted to the van rental burglary , the cars that were stolen and the petrol from cars in Hereford road .

Took Tim back to St Gilberts, spoke to staff that Tim would be confined to school until further notice and a review.

Court offence record for 26/05/83 for the above crimes.

Taking convenience without consent x 3, Aid and abet x 2, no insurance x 3, siphoning fuel, burglary to commercial premises x1, No Driving licence x 3.

25.4.83 Visit to St Gilberts

Collected Mrs Draycott to sit in at the review as soon as we arrived It was apparent that Tim wanted to stay at St Gilberts to take his C.S.E exams , he had no interest in going home in the near future , he admitted to stealing his sisters moped and the crimes that were mentioned at the police station and we agreed that I should speak to inspector Roach in relation to these so they can be taken into consideration when he attends court .

8.4.83

Visit to Mrs Draycott in hospital one fractured leg, possible road accident, phone StGilberts to inform them that Mrs Draycott was ok and no need to worry.

10.4.83 - Telephone call to StGilberts to let them know Timothys mother is being discharged before the weekend so timothy can visit , telephone call to Shrewsbury police Re Tim's driving ban and problem (?) , home visit to Allerton road to give Mrs Draycott bedding and sauce pans from the WRVS.

I have another few pages blanked off by social services here but not too long to jump to.

These blanked off pages I assume (by speaking to family) would be related to Mothers boyfriend who continued to beat her if provoked

23.4.83 - Telephone call from Shrewsbury police, Timothy has been in custody since the 22.4.83 and arrested for a taking and driving away (T.D.A) offence and some minor crimes with Tony Dodd, both boys to appear in a special magistrate court later in the day.

Timothy appeared in court and was charged with T.D.A, remanded in care until the 26.4.83.

Took Timothy back to StGilberts and discussed with staff about timothy having a residential care order under the criminal justice act, they were in agreement.

24.4.83. spoke to magistrates , police and St Gilberts in relation to everything being heard on the 26.4.83 , also regarding the residential care order , he will be heard by a special juvenile court sitting .

26.4.83. Timothy was sentenced to 6 months residential care order under the criminals justice act, returned to school by Peter Wakefield, social worker.

27.4.83 H.V to Allerton Road to explain the outcome of the court hearing, Mrs Draycotts boyfriend was also present at the address, Mrs Draycott says she will have nothing to do with Timothy and didn't want to see him again, I suggested that if she did not leave Tim alone as discussed last week that timothy would not have gone and committed the crimes with Tony, when he came home especially to look after his mother whilst she was poorly.

*She ignored that to speak to her boyfriend; she was discussing giving up the house to move back in with her boyfriend. (*More paragraphs are blanked off here).

I advised her to go and see Timothy as he would not be home for 6 months, this did not seem to worry her at all, and she said that she wouldn't want to go though.

Visited 26.4.83 to brothers houses to inform them what had happened and that they could visit.

8.6.83 – Arranged with Timothys sister to take her to see Tim the following Friday.

H.V to Allerton road , Mrs Draycotts boyfriend says she was feeling faint and could not come to the door , he Said she would feel comfortable and would not be able to accompany us the following Friday , I asked if she could contact me as soon as she is feeling unwell .

9.6.83 T.C to GP Sprake to Dr Tully who was not convinced that Mrs Draycott was ill and said that she had a long history of " fainting it" , should her condition deteriote or any recognisable symptoms show she would visit .

Telephone call to St Gilberts to confirm visit for the following week.

10.6.83. – Collected Sheryl and took her to St Gilberts (see separate file related to the details and conversation of this journey) Tim seemed in good spirits, a little awkward with Sheryl at first but was glad to see her, I left them alone whilst I spoke to staff, gave them a copy of the residential care order, I explained that I felt it best if timothy was kept away from the family for a while considering what was going on at his mothers.

I'm glad they did , I have many a paperwork on what I did for activities in these next months and I think some of the best times of my care life happened in these following months , I am going to mention some of these trips and the troubles we got on in them .

We went to London 3 times in the 3 years I was at St Gilberts , lucky I have many photos still of some of the places we visited due to my stolen Kodak camera.

I won't bore you with the Madame tussauds trip or the history museum , just look at photos on the internet as they haven't changed in 35 years (apart from Jason Donavan has gone).

I got a major clip around the ear on one London visit from one of our care workers for pissing up a side alley close to Trafalgar square , next to a pizza outlet , I'm sure the same visit as the photos above ?.

Wolverhampton ice rink 7.5.83, I met a girl on the rink and we hit it off , (this was also confirmed by my friend I visited a few weeks ago during corona lockdown , and no we did not socially distance), this girl was really pretty and all my mates did was have a go at her , I got warned from my care worker that I could do nothing as we were about to leave , I went outside with her and we started to snog behind a lorry , I kept looking out from the side to see if the team were coming out and we continued to snog until they did come out , care worker was looking around with a panic on his face but was ok when I came from behind the cab of the lorry , lads still taking the piss , probably jelous ?.

I lost count of the amount of times we went into wales, as mentioned the canoeing days were well and truly upon me and any excuse to get into the wild I would do.

30.6.83 *HV to Allerton road to arrange visit to see Timothy, Mrs Draycott now has her plaster off but is now having physiotherapy so she could not think of visiting as yet.*

T.C to St Gilberts they have explained that the others have had a long weekend into wales and are very tired , I did not want to let Timothy down so arranged that if either brother could not visit I would try Mrs Draycott again , called at Mrs Draycotts and she said she would try to get one of the brothers to visit.

I stole a newly brought out disc camera by Kodak, the film was expensive so I stole them as well, I had to pay for developing, they all wanted to play with it,

Andy if you remember you took these *(place emoji smiley thing here)*

These photos are from one of our trips to London, nice style of clothes then, you can see me, the lonely one who walked alone and sat alone.

You can also see a small can of beer in my mates hand , this was not unheard off , a way of keeping us subdued I suppose but I was not a drinker at the time (apart from nans whiskey , back in Shrewsbury)

Wow this is amazing I have come to page 138 out of 450 of my social workers reports for these 3 months leading to November and suddenly I turn the page and it's all in typewriter font , (I'm sure typewriters were invented before 1983 ?) this is truly amazing for me as its very hard to decipher what they are saying in previous reports , so in celebration of finding this unexpected glory in my life , here it is compared to the previous page , this means I can rest my tired typing fingers as you can read this yourself but as I like writing I will get back onto it , this is not good , I cannot find my camera that takes the good shots of my paperwork , I am sure I have given it to a friend for her daughters college assailment , so I'm going to have to use my laptop camera , which is pretty shit but at least it comes away from the keyboard , no that was shit so now I'm going to try my camera phone .

That's better , look at the quality on that , I'm getting good at this book photo thing , I think I might take it up I've got a good idea about a popup book about a talking lorry called Laurie.

Name Draycott Timothy Case Paper No. C2412/3
(Surname first Block letters)

REPORT BY	Initials
of the residential order trying, and was asking when he could spend a day at home. Explained this would not be for a while at least, but we would look into some form of home contact towards the end of the order. However I reminded him that we would have to get this authorised by the court. One day he would like at home is when Melanyn's baby is christened, but as Liz hasn't had the baby yet that isn't an urgent problem. Mrs Draycott will try to get to see Tim either under her own steam or with Tony or Malin but I will take her down anyway next time I go.	
[illegible signature]	

Date	REPORT BY	Initials
26.7.83.	Collected Mrs Draycott and took her down to St. Gilberts to see Tim. Tim had absconded from the school shortly after we had visited the previous time and had returned to the camp in Wales where he had been with the school. He was found by other members of staff with another group of boys and returned to the school. There were no offences. Tim had settled into the school again following his abscoation and there were no real problems. Staff were however concerned about the problem of home contact as Tim is beginning to find the residential order very irksome. Discussed with Peter Wakefield and Mrs Draycott and Tim the possibilities of him having some home leave and the terms of the residential order and it was agreed that I would look into the possibilities of this as we may need to go back to the Magistrates. It was also agreed that we would try and arrange a day visit for Tim to see the baby when Liz has had it. This however will not be until the end of August as I am away on leave and then with the school holidays there will not be sufficient staff available to make arrangements for Tim to come up for the day. It was agreed that Mrs Draycott would notify me when the baby was born and I would make arrangements sometime after the week ending 22nd August for Tim to come up for the day.	
29.7.83.	Message from Mrs Draycott to say that Liz had had a little boy Sam.	
15.8.83.	Abortive home visit to Mrs Draycott.	

15.8.83.	Abortive home visit to Mrs Draycott.
17.8.83.	Abortive home visit to Mrs Draycott.
18.8.83.	Home visit to Melvyn Draycott. Melvyn was at work but I spoke to Liz who is happy for Tim to come up and see them sometime next week. She is now home with the baby and everything seems to be fine.

Third party information

| 22.8.83. | Home visit to Liz at Crowwsole Lane. |

Made arrangements for Tim to visit on Wednesday. I will collect him from St. Gilberts and take him to his mothers and then bring him and his mother round to Liz's later in the afternoon before returning him to St. Gilberts. Liz is quite happy with this arrangement.

| 24.8.83. | Collected Timothy from St. Gilberts and delivered him to his mothers. Left Draycotts for half an hour while I did another visit then collected him and |

Date	REPORT BY	Initi
cont'd..	his mother and dropped them off at Mrs Hargreaves. After lunch I collected them again and took them to Melvyn's flat and left them there for the afternoon. I returned later in the afternoon but Timothy persuaded me to allow him to stay a bit longer so he could see Melvyn when he came in from work. Returned later in the afternoon after Melvyn had returned and then collected Tim and his Mum and took them back to St. Gilberts. Everyone was very keen for Tim to start having weekends at home again, but I explained that we were still dependant on the courts agreement. During the course of the day I had an opportunity to talk to Tim about his future plans, in particular the Youth Training Scheme he is supposed to be doing. He said that he did not want to do a Youth Training Scheme anymore, but I did not have the opportunity to go into the reasons for this.	

Collected Mrs Draycott and took her down to visit Timothy. We had some discussion with Timothy and a member of staff regarding his lack of enthusiasm for Youth Training Scheme. After considerable discussion it appears that Timothy's main objection was that he didn't want to be involved in building work which he seemed to think was the only option. Once we explained to him that there were various alternatives available under the Youth Training Scheme he was more enthusiastic and it was agreed that arrangements would be made by St. Gilberts for Tim to see the Careers Officer. He was particularly interested in a fibreglassing job. We talked again about the possibility of having weekend leave, but until we hear from the court we cannot make these arrangements as it may well be that the court may feel that they do not want Timothy to have weekend leave until the end of the order given the circumstances under which the order was made. Mrs Draycott would like to visit Timothy under her own steam whilst I am away on leave, but has not been able to get a warrant from the Social Security. We may be able to help her with a travel warrant ourselves.

Telephone call to St. Gilberts to check on the progress of Timothy's careers appointment. He has not in fact seen the careers officer yet but this is in hand. St. Gilberts will notify me when they have any definite news.

13.9.83. Timothy's position discussed with the magistrates at Juvenile Panel Meeting. It seemed quite clear that although the order was made at a time when Timothy was at home and unsupervised it was not their intention that he should have no home contact and they accept the view that Timothy should have home contact toward the later part of the order. We will now be able to plan ahead and arrange a programme of weekend leaves for the later part of

Oh that's just great, turn the page and this is what I get, a little insy bitsy bit of type then they must have taken the typewriter from her (Maggie Thatcher's Government cuts?)

SHROPSHIRE COUNTY COUNCIL —SOCIAL SERVICES COMMITTEE

Name: __Timothy Draycott__   Case Paper No. C.2412/3
(Surname first
Block letters)

Date	REPORT BY	Initials
cont'd..	the order. I will notify St. Gilberts and we will make arrangements when I return from leave.	
15.9.83	T/C to St Gilberts to notify Ken re above and arranged to visit on 3.10.83	
5.10.83	Not able to visit T/C to St Gilberts to rearrange visit for 12.10.83 Called to see Mrs Draycott to advise her of change of plans. She had visited Tim during my absence using the travel warrant we provided. When I visited Mrs Draycott she informed	

I have had to cut it short as the social services have failed to omit my mother's boyfriend's name which was very naughty of them; I'm not allowed to see that.

But I do like a reference further below which I cannot put in; saying that Mrs Draycotts boyfriend with regret has come back on the scene.

But you can see what I mean about the writing to type format, aggh and it so carries on so another month of me trying to decipher.

I will go over some of the comments made in the reports above though just to clear up any questions you may have on it.

I was showing a keen interest in the fibre glassing as I was making my own canoes at St Gilberts whilst I was on the kids prison care order and to tell you the truth I loved the smell of the resin, high – you don't know what it is ice to be high unless you fibreglass a canoe with no mask on (but I do hear you lose around 20,000 brain cells when taking poppers, that amol nitrate stuff), I'm sure you would lose more brain cells taking resin.

I was interested to see the paragraph on me absconding and returning to the campsite in wales, this was on my own accord and I actually went legally on the train from Hartlebury with back pack and all the stuff you take when doing a runner on a residential care order.

The camp we went on a few weeks prior was on the banks of the dolgethlhi river, a lonely place on a disused mill pond, this is where I honed my skills at Eskimo rolling and escapism from the canoe if submerged, the canoe hut was in the middle of know where, the only items apart from a shabby shed was the log pile which I think the farmer stocked due to us ripping off branches from the old trees on the previous visits

I got to this site by simply bus and train , walked many miles inside the hedgerow on my own , I didn't have to much care when it came to timings , no rush to get anywhere in a hurry if you're on the run , (your thinking why I was on the run well wait a moment , I will get to it).

I arrived to see a couple of camps already set up next to the river so I made my way to the opposite hill then overlooked the valley, maybe I could steal the minibus or some provisions as I really could not stay at that place, I thought I was just going to break into the shed, grab a canoe and paddle down to the sea, I could then go anywhere in the world.

I heard before I seen the lad shouting aloud and I knew straight away it was my ole mucka from Shrewsbury Besford house, I could tell his voice from a mile away (I was not far away though), I knew he was in Besford after Detention centre where he was supposed to be a good boy due to his father accepting him back now he had remarried.

Fuck that , I went down , casually walked into the campsite with my backpack on as if I was a hiker , walked right through it when the fire was lit and all sitting around it , I could not see him , I must have been mistaken .

I got accosted by an adult who followed me to the river fence saying I was young to be walking this time at night as I was about to get over a sty, as learnt from my protégée I told him to fuck off as I knew he was some sort of care worker, I then heard my old friends voice shouting my name and laughing, "Oh great "I was soon back at St Gillies.

I also notice a reference that I hated building and I did indeed when I was younger , later in life (3 years later) I was No 1 bricklayer in youth custody centre (3 sentences on the trot) and even now during lockdown (July 2020) I am out and about building patios , driveways , putting up shelves and generally enjoying myself as I am not governed by the rules the government has set out – I'm a builder (and hopefully a misspelled autobiographist)

I see nothing but squabbling on the reports now between my mother and father through my social workers writing, my brothers and sisters welfare seemed to be good also, my social worker had a very busy time with my family whilst I was enjoying myself around the country, this carries on for a month on the reports, my father saying he now has opportunities for me in thatching and maybe going abroad with him as my mother was well and truly stuck with her new abusive boyfriend,

My social worker seemed happy that me and my father has made friends again , my brothers would take my mother's boyfriend down a peg or two (which they did) just like they did with the previous ruffian a couple of years prior , all good so far as I was adamant that I wanted to visit Shrewsbury .

("I explained to Tim that his mother was not offering him a place at hers at the moment and that he should find alternative places just stay at St Gilberts or go to his fathers, I explained to Tim that I would help on this by visiting his brothers in the coming days) . (Thanks mum).

Do I feel bitter on my mother for the previous 5 years of non caring for me – not at all , I loved my mother and father and I would have regardless of what they did or said about me .

Some of you may think "what he doing here a diary "well no I'm not, I think this is a big turning point in my life and for a few pages it was worth telling and still is, so I'm going to carry on for the moment in social services format (as they tell it better in the 80s) and filling in where I remember – I hope you don't mind?.

.28.10.83 – HV to Mrs Draycott , she has asked if I could arrange a transfer to another house , I explained that she would need to stay in Allerton road for 1 year to be eligible for a transfer but I would ask for her .

My life and my mother's life is massively blanked off here for a whole page and I really wish I could see this but I must assume that her boyfriend had beaten her, I think this is when my brothers intervened, my sister was on subject in a paragraph of a care order., we were really a spread out family at that time.

I think mainly they all left the house due to my mother's cooking , She would cook rice in abundance , for breakfast , dinner and tea , oh and pudding from the left over .

"Oh just bung some milk on it and stick it in the oven "= Yes mum (rice pudding that would make Jamie Oliver weep)

This is a wonderful part of the book for me as nothing is written about me for nearly a month , sorry just had another look as I found that unbelievable that social services or the police have nothing on me from the 28th oct – 16th Nov , this means I must have been a good boy for these 3 weeks , stayed at St Gillies and got myself prepped for c.s.e's and my future Y.T.S scheme I suppose , so as I'm oblivious to what happened to that 3 weeks I will jump straight to my statutory review .

If you think I'm turning over a new leaf at this point in my life, you are completely wrong.

It gets worse and worse and worse.

You can skip a chapter here though as it's not as interesting as chapter 12 & 16 but better than 8 & 4, but on par with 2 & 20 (maybe 5 as well).

Chapter 22rd

(The last 20, 000 words Chapter or "the long" chapter).

16.11.83. – statutory review of Timothy took place at St Gilberts, we did before the review Timothys options with him and he told me he had applied for and got in a Y.T.S scheme at a local furniture shop, he was very pleased with this and said to staff that he would like to remain at St Gilberts and pursue this rather than going home to Mrs Draycotts.

Mrs Draycott was very much against this saying if Tim was old enough to work then he was old enough to go home.

Timothy could not say directly to his mother that he preferred to stay at the school, he ended up in tears trying to tell his mother and left the room, we decided to review the situation in 3 months after Tim has started the course at the shop.

Now at this point according to my reports I was refused to work at the furniture shop as Mr Carter said he had boys from the home before as they were not trustworthy.

My mother was trying to get a travel warrant 2 days after seeing me , I think to come back and persuade me to transfer to Shrewsbury after my residential care order (R.C.O) finished mid November , wow not long until I can decide what I wanted to do for the rest of my life .

On the blessing of a care worker I went from St Gilberts and half walked, half bus the 6 miles into Kidderminster to Carters Furniture warehouse and spoke to the salesman who said Mr Carter was not around and he was in charge, so I left a message to see if I could have an interview with Mr Carter as I was not like the others from the home.

I had a good long chat with this fella, after giving him the message and leaving I didn't see him again?

My Enquiry reports state on the 21.11.83 that the shop rang St Gilberts and asked if I could start the following week for 3 days a week.

Yes I know what you readers are thinking, "wow this Tim (me, the writer) bloke is amazing, so much spunk "at 15 years old

But really, whatever that salesman said got me the job.

Carters furniture warehouse in kiddermister was a funny old place Mr Carter the owner was a really nice bloke, always had time for you, I don't think the trust was there at first as he knew I came from a naughty boys home but as he was getting a near freebie on my YTS scheme and I think he really trusted me, I got the job, I don't know why as I was shaking really mad when I arrived for my first day and as an afterthought his wife was a stunner for her age.

My task at first was to just tidy up, dust the showroom furniture for 3-ish weeks, I think Mr Carter had hopes for me to sell furniture and be a salesman? , just like the pretentious twat who was doing it at the time, he was so smarmy, yuppies not invented yet but you get my drift.

I think this led to me hating salesmen with their polished suits and ties, when I was in life, was a "ruffian ".

Within a week I was making headboards from scratch in the back store room, cutting the chipboard with a jigsaw, then plush upholstery, but the back and the filling was crap chip wood and foam, I did the buttons, pleats, filling the clothe back, stapling the whole thing together and then just before I left I did the shop assistant who was working at the time as a p/t secretary.

This relationship did not go far (a month maybe) apart from some very polite foreplay in the warehouse; I fell deeply and madly in love with her after that.

I brought her Toto's record Rosanna and (I left the raaaains down in Africaaaaaa record, I don't think she was impressed, I still love it and its on my Amazon playlist, I will never buy again thought, ha - don't need to with Amazon music, I don't think she brought me anything but I did not need anything, I just needed her.

I would have given up the life of crime for her but I was 2 years her junior and I had to go back to naughty boys home straight after so no chance in meeting in the evening ever.

 You don't get much chance to meet the young ladies whilst in boys homes all of your young adult life ,they are mainly ball lifting dinner ladies or house masters (yes ,some wanted to be the woman) ,housemasters wives or even boys at homes who wanted to be girls and ask to suck your dick to see what it was like , but we now live in a trans thingy , non binary , bisexualism world type world , I still do not understand even though I lived in London for 12 years going out to gay nightclubs ,bars and secret door clubs (wink wink) in the 90s/00s , give or take a year and when I had my own catering company , which reminds me catering in my own business later in life for one of the cast members of a very popular TV programme , a wedding event , I'm sure every guest was transgender neutral binary guests?, but we left with my bar manager in shock that he touched a gorgeous ladies bollock .

At that event in 2012 we left at 2am in Cheltenham after my bar staff was approached to engage in that sexual activity with the he/she lady man.

Sorry nearly going off track again so this girl at Carters was different , I did honestly fall in love with her , 17 years old , blonde hair , girl next door face , a very nice figure and most importantly she was as honest as fuck , unbelievably she did not lie at all .

I was also honest at Carters furniture warehouse, I never stole a thing (Ha , I could not walk out with a double bed or sideboard can I)and I was always as polite as I could be but Carters is still going strong , they have built many buildings around it but I went past a few weeks ago to still see the logo on the building , I would pop down there if I were you and see if they have any headboards , I can vouch for them as obviously the trade for headboard making would have been passed on by me probably .

Let's not hope you meet the salesman whose trade has not been passed on from the bloke in the 80s, seriously- good honest family run business that have quality furniture and... Staff.

13.12.83 – Phone call to St Gilberts Kinver unit , Tim still very much enjoying his work at the furniture warehouse but very disgruntled about his home leave , threatening to do what he likes to staff , I have arranged a visit for the following week , after his weekend at home he has come back saying his mother is now back with her abusive boyfriend , he was rather upset about this and insisted he was going home this weekend , I mentioned that the residential order was now finished and we could discuss this but Christmas is very soon and he will have loads of time in Shrewsbury with family .

16.12.83 – Big Blank offs here again so I assume again it is to do with my mother and boyfriend, but I suppose I will never know?

So into a new year, not a lot to say in my reports apart from how well I'm doing at the furniture place, how I enjoyed my home visit, my sister is living in my mother's house which the social worker describes as a mess and in quite a state (naughty sister), mum has broke up with her abusive partner again (that's the 4th Time).

I was then carrying on with my furniture upholstery and assembly, and I tell you what some of the assemblies brought over from foreign lands were pretty damn hard when trying to decipher Chinese or Indian, so some of the times when I was Assembling I made up my own designs and redid, filled in the area, and I tell you what again, I was pretty damn good at hiding mistakes that I had done,.

My main line I used to say at that time that " it wasn't me " shrugged my shoulders and walked away , I also kept that going through my early catering days .

I was then enrolled in the local tech studying retail and distribution , this was for 3 days a week and I would jump on to the furniture shop on the Saturday to make up my Y.T.S scheme .

They decided at the school to let me go from the independent Kinver unit into my own chalet type building called Malvern , as the lads in the school were a bit young for me to associate with and that I really should be independent now   , but I still had to apply for this unit , apparently I was reluctant to move in and I did have discussions about this to the staff member who picked me up after college one night when I was housed in Malvern , I think moving me was a ploy to shut me up and keep me out of the way of the abuser and when I did have my meeting with my old friend from St Gillies , he mentioned my driver as an abuser (yeah 2 and 2 = , and all that).

My college days I hated , all I wanted to do was go down the chippy under the viaduct and doss out , it was boring , I didn't get on with any of the pretentious twats that attended , basically I was not a college boy and I didn't want to be .

24.1.84. I remember this well.

Timothy has been playing a practical joke on all staff , he fills a whiskey bottle with cold tea and either offers it to staff or pretends to be drunk and asleep on the floor , staff think Tim also has a girlfriend as he comes back to the unit full of spirit and tells stories at the dinner table .

My files go on to say in this month about my mother now staying at my grandmothers and my sister being idle at Mums house with her friend, same old same old not tidying, uninterested in finding work or even to give mother the house back, My sisters social worker has found her a place to stay in the next month though, so all is well.

Too late for my mother though as she was warned a possession order was going to be made, so mother gave up the house and reapplied for another, which she got within a couple of weeks by the looks of it on my reports, (crafty mother), she now resides in Cockayne Green (a house I remember so so well) my sister went to move into a flat with her friend so all was well.

I was living it up in St Gilberts n the month of January , working at the furniture showroom and doing college every day , going home for weekends to grandmothers and amazingly about to take more courses and join a squash club , become an official table official for the BBF (British basketball federation) .

What could go wrong (I'm sure I have said that before)?

Carters said they would not be offering me a full time job after my Y.T.S course had finished which would be the following week, I was going to miss Carters furniture store for the fun times, I often think back on that part of my employment life and ponder that it was a good part of my life, not as good as my next employment though.

I seem to have jumped into a second job straight away at a food store called Lo-Cost food stores In Kidderminster, just a little off the high street, these youth training scheme people certainly did the job, back then Maggie was pushing for the unemployed to get off their asses as I think it was bordering on 3 million unemployed (excuse me if I'm wrong, I do not want to be the spreader of fake news).

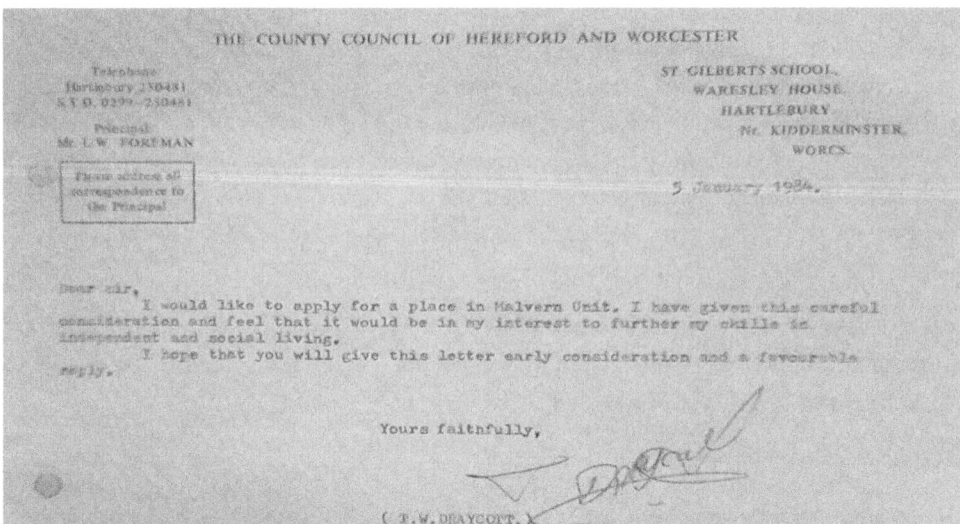

31st January, 1984

Timothy Draycott,
St. Gilberts School,
Hartlebury,
Worcs.

Dear Timothy,

Further to your visit and telephone call to this office today,
we confirm that we have spoken by telephone to Carters Furnishings
and Low-Cost Stores.

Your date of leaving Carters will be this Friday, 3rd February,84
and your starting date at Low-Cost Stores, Monday 6th February,84.

Hope the move proves satisfactory.

Yours sincerely,

Cherill Mason

Mrs Cherrill Mason
Secretary to Y.T.S. Training Officer.

7.2.84, Timothy has now moved his job to a Tuesday, Wednesday and Saturday causing a few problems for weekend leave, I have phoned St Gilberts to express my concerns after Timothy refused to speak to me.

28.2.84 , Could not visit Tim prior to today due to bad weather and the school being snowed in , went to visit today and Tim was in high spirits , he has now moved into the Malvern unit where he is expected to look after himself , he is obliged to save a weekly sum and if he stays in the unit he would be expected to pay a small rent , he says his aim is to buy a motorcycle , I have agreed to look into if he is still banned , I told Tim that Mr Draycott says he has no room but this did not phase Tim at all , it is very clear that Tim does not see a future in Kidderminster and is keen to get back to Shrewsbury when his order is complete , I explained this would not be a problem but we would have to find a suitable accommodation .

1.3.1984, - Checked with the Magistrates and it seems that Tim's driving convictions have expired, T/C to StGilberts to relay the message.

I'm going to Break away from the social reports to tell you a bit about Lo-cost food stores I think , as it was quite influential to me and my working life , I was mainly behind closed doors at Carters but this was different , I had to interact with normal people , people who lived in the outside world .

I will tell you it was a frightening experience for me , I've kicked coppers , railway guards , had fights with school teachers and all other bad things in life but this was different , I had to talk to people , people who did not know anything about my past , what I had done and what I was capable of .

It was a small supermarket , 3 isles , 2 small checkouts but only 1 was ever manned , I would say grubby on the floor and in the warehouse, shabbily (is that a word ?)Placed items on the shelves, 5 shelves high, nothing in any real order, the beans could be next to the cat food and bread next to the artichoke hearts.

The Manager was a young bloke who really did not have a clue about anything , I ended up telling him about impulse buys and the general layout of the store , I think I was invaluable as I had been at college now a few months studying all this .

I was general dogsbody for the first few weeks or so and then got promoted to tills and shop assistant, wow what a step up from being Shropshire biggest prolific car thief to a near shop manager.

As I was on £15 pw and from that a rent of £9 pw , transport to work , lunch at college (making me fatter) , I was broke and they still expected me to save £2.00 pw but I had my bike to think of , so I had to save .

That means I also had to steal, and steal I did, not so much for me but for another shop assistant who always came in late and left early as she had a child, she was around 25-30.

I'm not sure if I can mention her name as she may read this and I would not like any bad press on the woman but my god was she a slut, she asked me to take some things out for her as he bag got checked and she was nervous about these things.

So like the gullible mule I was I agreed, this kept on for a while, virtually every time I was in the shop.

It was minor items, basically a food parcel box, no more than £3 worth of items but very useful if you are skint, I did on some occasions place a luxury item in the box as I did with my box I started to make up and place by the dumpster at the back of the shop.

This progressed to me making up a larger box and going to her council house at the top of the hill, a long trek for me, out of my way but worth it when I got there, her kid was about 5/6, her house was cheaply furnished, mainly hand me downs but she managed to get a 3 bedroom house from the council, fair play to her as you cannot get that now.

Her boyfriend she said had left her and I'm not surprised as on 2 occasions when I went to her house she virtually shooed me away as she was either drunk or had a bloke in the house.

I asked her in the back warehouse what am I going to get in return for all these favours I'm doing for her (I highly suppose sexual innuendos would have be involved in the conversation), I would find out later when I went to her house, after the usual 5pm drink, I don't know how it came about but she took my pants down and started to stroke me.

I didn't bat an eyelid my hands where down her top squeezing them large bosoms and before I knew it on her balooma, we were having a whale of a time before her daughter asked what she was doing, bloody hell did I shoot up, my jeans around my ankles, her blouse top all undone and her skirt up to her waist.

That same week I caught her walking past the shop with a bloke, I knew then that she was either too old for me or was using me to get stolen food to her.

We carried on with the foreplay in the warehouse but never did we have sex or indeed make love and I very nearly fell in love with her, we stopped seeing each other in the warehouse when she got into a ramshackle of a car and I questioned her over it, it was her kids father, the same kids father who hit her and went out with her best friend.

After that for a few weeks she seemed prim and proper at work, her hair looked good and she had a glow in her skin, I don't think that was down to a lad 10 years her junior, but I feel like I did help her, she then just left, no sight or sound of her, I had no reason to go to her house as the parcels stopped when I could not go to her house again.

What I thought was because of her daughter finding us on the floor but it was really the copious amounts of men she was using to get what she wanted.

Her hair was paid for by an old bloke who lived opposite to her, her new clothes from another bloke who used to wait sometime outside the shop, he took her clothes shopping.

Another bloke who picked her up Saturday and the boyfriend who came to the shop to argue with her, yep the girl was a user and in my eyes at the time and now a proper slut, I think I learnt from her, yes I would have learnt from her, maybe subliminally but I learnt, so if your reading this, Thank you slut.

I went up to assistant isle manager , no rise in wages just another fancy name as we had an assistant manager , manager , till manager , till assistant manager that's 4 plus me , only us 5 worked in the shop ?.

5.3.84 , - T/C to St Gilberts to ask how Tim got on with his weekend visit to be told that Timothy had rung up to say he had flue , this was understandable as I also have been feeling flu symptoms .

6.3.84 , - T/C to St Gilberts to ask if Tim had arrived they informed me that he had but arrived back on his mothers motorcycle which they have locked up or until Tim receives his licence , he would be uninsured and I was informed no tax on the motorcycle .

8.3.84 , - T/C from Mrs Draycott saying she wanted her motorcycle back , I advised her that she should not have given it to Tim as he was not legal , Mrs Draycott agreed to go to the school to collect the bike , Mrs Draycott also explained that she has been given the tenancy for cockayne green house and that her daughter would be moving in with her as she cannot afford the rent on her flat , agree with the school that Tim should be reviewed 28.3.84 with the prospect of moving back to Shrewsbury and to transfer the Y.T.S scheme .

A visit to my mother's new house by my social worker brought up a surprise as her violent boyfriend was present along with my sister who spoke to Mrs waring about me not living at my father's as he was so strict, my mother offered to take me in weekends but could not control me as I did what I liked anyway, my father agreed to take me in but with conditions, what conditions I do not know?.

I feel like I know a lot about this time in my life, I remember the visits to the probation office, I remember the walk home every day from the store, even down to the impulse buys next to the shop till, but as mentioned one thing I do remember is this house in cockayne green and the future cars I would steal and abandon on the school field or pub car park very close to the green, (not too long to wait for them stories).

Enough of home let's get back to my days in St Gilberts in these months around my birthday as it seems I accomplished a lot and threw it all away .(as usual).

I was due to be released form St Gilberts in less than 2 months and I'm sure it was worrying me , as mentioned I was taking as many courses I could so all will be ok with my qualifications when I got back to Shrewsbury surely ? .

6.4.84 , I only got myself motorbike from a motorbike shop in Kiddy , amazingly on credit agreement which my grandmother gave her guarantee that I would pay (a year later she paid for me due to me defaulting on the agreement) , a yammy DT50 , I could drive this on my provisional , I was all legal , apart from insurance and tax , but who checks them , as long as I had learner plates on I wouldn't get pulled over surely ?.

St Gilberts in their usual self banned me from using it but didn't lock it up like my mother's moped and at the first instance I stole it back and parked it down the farm in a hidden corner in a barn, Ha, they didn't even notice that it had gone from the back of the main house, I did get it legal by the 15th so I didn't have long to wait, I just didn't like the idea of them keeping it when I am supposed to be an individual now.

I started to give my things away at this point , all my star wars toys (approx 200-ish)went to a lad in the main house , these I swapped for the full collection of Smurfs , I bet he is smiling now , all the posh clothes I had stolen over the past few years (tacchini , la'cost ,farrah etc)also went to lads in the main house , whatever I could not fit on my bike went to the lads in the main house .

I took a trip to the careers office in Kidderminster and followed it up with a trip (on my motorbike) to my social worker to ask about what my options are about employment in Shrewsbury and would I get help with any benefits if I cannot find work, according to my reports she did the best she could by getting me an appointment with the careers office in Shrewsbury and after that an interview with a local Company (supermarket assistant).

On the 16th April 1984 I travelled the long tedious journey doing 40mph all the way to Shrewsbury , I smiled all the way , I was nearly free , the shop dummy which tony was beating up being the funniest day of my life , this being the most smiliest .

I was back at St Gilberts that night getting ready to leave in the next few days.

So 11am the morning of the 20th April 1984 I loaded saddle bags on my bike, a massive rucksack on my back, a load of tears being dished out as I was doing this, I went to see as many staff as I possibly could, even down the squash court to see the local residents (it was empty) so hardly any staff to say so long to it was time to leave.

A very sad day for me indeed, I had accomplished so much here and I would probably never see anyone again, a part of me didn't want to go but I did.

Chapter 18 (Home time)

I got the job , it was at a small supermarket at the edge of Shrewsbury , I really cannot mention the name as the man who owns (owned) it is still very much an influential man in Shrewsbury but this place was a dive , far worse than Lo-cost , I could go into detail but I will mention one instance .

A packet of 250g suet mix on the shelf , I was doing a stock rotate , this means the nearly out of date items come to the front and just delivered go to the back (so always take your food from the back of the shelf) I picked up a box from the front and all underneath was mold , green and hairy , me being a young shop assistant I took this to the owner , where as he wiped the mold off and gave it me back to put on the shelf , I explained it might be inside , so he took it back opened the box , poured the contents on the table , wiped inside the box , placed the items back in the box , put some glue on the cardboard and gave it me back to put on the shelf , even then I really did think you dirty fucker and I still do when I see him or his brother trouncing around town , disgusting .

No I've changed my mind I'm telling you another instance , local lady leaving her change on the side , I notice this so put my box down and went to get the money to take out to her , Mr shop owner picked it up , didn't count it and put it in the till , I explained to him that it was that ladies change but he said she would come back in if she noticed it missing , he was the most anus of bosses , in all my working life I have never met such a self centred , pretentious knob rot than him .

I am happy to say that I left after a couple of weeks, I walked out as he shouted at me and then low and behold the shop closed a few months later, I'm really not surprised, but this left me in limbo about finishing off my college which I transferred to Shrewsbury from kiddermister and I only had a month left on my Y.T.S.

I hated Shrewsbury college all I did all day was stare out of the window and it was bad enough to say this to my social worker, she tried to talk me out of finishing early a few times by the looks of it, I was unemployed, no money as I was too young to apply for anything so the only thing I could turn to was either ringing the cars again or some shoplifting, a few weeks later it would be all three on my criminal record.

Looks like I'm on the slippery slope to be either institutionalized or having a life of unsolved crimes which I was about to commit (but get caught for in the end).

I was jumping around staying at brothers, mothers, grandmothers and fathers; I had no base until my sister moved into her own house and had a spare room.

My mother was back with her abusive boyfriend , grandmother was asking me for enema's to loosen up her bottom area all of the time to the point in offering me money constantly to place this tube up her bum , luckily my brothers girlfriend was a nurse and took on the duty of the squirt , but it would not be to long until I lost my grandmother so I did my best to look after her in-between my general dossing around doing nothing , staying at friends house my father told my social worker and it happened very often in the month of May 84.

I went back to St Gilberts on the 1.6.84 , my reports state it was because I was lonely and a bit lost in what to do in Shrewsbury and that would be my refuge , I do remember going back and luckily a member of staff that looked after me for a few years was present , I spoke to him in-depth about my life in Shrewsbury , I broke down in front of him and like the good bloke he was (and still is)he consoled me and gave me the confidence to go back to Shrewsbury , I really did not want to , no one wanted me , and I am not saying that for the sympathy vote , it says it in my reports " *Tim says he feels alone in Shrewsbury and is finding it hard to find work and friends who do not encourage him to cause trouble* ".

This is when I got very zitty, I was covered in them by the age of 17, never a real problem before but this zit problem would be so bad that the following year when I was on a prison sentence they requested a special Doctor to see me and he prescribed me special drugs to combat it, me being a very touchy face type person I carried on squeezing the little blighters, even though my face was like I had jaundice covering it due to the magnolia colour of the zit cream.

I was generally dossing going to our local youth club at Belmont , still very much a community hub after all these years , free coffee , pool as long as we did our bit in doing the garden or a touch of painting , always happy to help out at Belmont and a bonus my dentist was next door which at the time I went to regularly but since then I have not paid a trip to a dentist , I got paranoid when that same dentist hurt me badly enough to make my mouth bleed all day , I went back the following day to give him back the filling plaster stuff which fell out the previous evening , bodge artist.

I was riding my motorbike with a friend on the back , we both had helmets but the police were content in stopping me , I was to have none of it and got chased as far as they could chase me along the river to get to Castlefields , we got apprehended just coming into Castlefields as the copper jumped out and grabbed me as I was about to take a corner , good ole copper had me well and truly banged to rights , he grabbed my key so I grabbed his jacket so much that when he stepped back me and my passenger fell of the bike and the bike landed on top of us , he was not too pleased , my passenger was though as the copper told him to go , I was a wanted man by the police , they all knew me and they all wanted my name on their paperwork " *yeah we caught Timothy Draycott*"

I was then to realise I was not a juvenile anymore and they pressed charges , No L plates , No insurance and not qualified to carry a pillion passenger ,my first crime since being a juvenile.

It was not the only crime though that would be bestowed on me when I went to court the following month.

8.7.84, - *Timothy came in to talk about his employment options and that he has know here to live as his mother has now moved in with her boyfriend again, he told me that his mum has asked him to leave by the following week and that he must find a flat, I have agreed to* speak to Mrs Draycott this week and speak to the council about any upcoming accommodation.

10.7.84 , -H/V I spoke to Mrs Draycott and she agreed that she would attend the review on the 18th , H/V To Mr Draycott who also agreed to visit on the 18th in regard to starting work abroad with himself

18.7.84, - Timothy arrived for his review, his mother and father failed to attend as promised, he was very jovial and seemed happy to just drift along until he found a job, he said like his brothers did at his age, he was not really concerned about the upcoming charges, he came on his motorcycle which he insisted was insured and taxed, I very much doubt it was though.

I was given my summons on the 9/8/84 to attend court on the 23rd of that month , I went to the social services again on my illegal bike to ask if they would help out on this and to say what a nice boy I was that I had turned over a new leaf , she says in her reports that she will do her best , I mentioned to her that I would sell my motorcycle to lead a new life and that I could not afford to run it , she did agree with me .

She mentioned that I was going to work at our local (famous)flower show for £10 per day which was a very nice wage , all I did for them 2 days from 8am-7pm was to fill small paper bags with Quick fry , these are basically quavers or prawn crackers made on the spot in hot oil , they just sizzle up in the oil, pretty amazing to watch (and eat) , the bloke who did them was making a killing as they were new on the scene , you could buy a box of the pressed square cut maize and fry them yourself , even better the following year he brought along coloured versions , I remember my elder brother getting me that job as I think he did it the previous year but I'm sure he will correct me when if he gets this far in reading my 80,000 million trillion word memoir .

Will it ever end I hear you cry out, well due to my next 7 youth custody sentences over the next 4 years, 3 prison sentences for 2 years after that and a baby thrown in, I really cannot answer that as yet, I have another 200 pages of social enquiry reports to go through, countless police reports explaining my crimes, court dates and later life minor activity, so I ponder to myself how to end this book as the title mentions "into the arms of the carers".

I am thinking of writing a follow up book " Out of the arms of the carers " , this will go through my later prison life from the age of 21 , my new born child , then suddenly into being a back of house manager working at prestigious events like Wimbledon , Royal Ascot , The Derby , The Grand prix , The Open golf , the world cup rugby and many many more .

The meeting , dining and having laughs with celebrities like Bob Monkhouse , James brown , Nigel Man sell , oh the list is massive and I have a story to tell or two and even catering for her majesty the Queen and Margaret Thatcher, I could write another novel on what really went on at the opening of the Eurotunnel and Silverstone 98 ?.

(Addition - Oct 2020, Second book started)

So I am now in my book life nearly out of the arms of the carers unless you think youth custody or prison are carers , they are and they are not , to me they are not , I go on the belief that when you pass the age of 18 you should no longer be under anyone's care , I realise this is difficult now but then you simply signed on with the local council and bang 6-12 months later you are housed , now we live in a multi cultural country which is at a crises point because it is mainly money orientated so the youth of today don't really have the step up's that we had , I think I wasted some of these opportunities that were given to me but some I took on board like the basket ball certificate's , the tournament squash playing , and all the awards I achieved at St Gilberts and in courses in the various prisons.

But fear not, you still have a bit more of a chapter of gruel to read and then I have to go back through it and add so much as I have either found more pages from my social services muddled up in all the other paperwork, the police have sent me what I have requested or I have thought of more memories after a memory jog.

22.9.84 , - Timothy came into the office to say that he has a chance to go away with the youth club and would it be possible to write a letter to court to plead guilty to his driving offences , I wrote as letter on his behalf and got him to sign it , it was sent to the clerk the same day

23.9.84 , - T/C from the clerk of the court to say he had received the letters , he could not understand Timothys hang writing , he mentioned that times sentence for the driving offence was a £30.00 fine and £3.00 costs , I phoned Tim's mother to relay the message

24.9.84 , - T/C from Shrewsbury police , Timothy has been arrested over the weekend with an old friend , he has admitted to taking a motor vehicle , he will appear in a special court tomorrow .

I was remanded in custody for 2 weeks which was not nice as this was the first time I had been in an adult prison The Dana, Shrewsbury.

This was a fantastic place; I loved every minute apart from Tarlochan (Tar-Lo-Shan)

I think I knew a majority of the screws as most of them either lived in Castlefields within a few hundred yards of my fathers , they knew my mother or family members who had previously been incarcerated at her majjies pleasure .

I shall not name the screws as they are very much still alive but my mother used to smuggle to them half Oz of rolling tobacco and this would get passed to me , I still did not smoke at this time so all good contraband I could get I would sell to get what I wanted .

My first term at the Dana was forgettable , my second time however was unforgettable , Totally jumping a year here but as I will not be getting that far in this memoir I'm going to tell you about this.

Every new inmate was placed on watch for 1 night in a special single cell , cardboard chair , table and no sharp objects and until they found me a space on the remand wing (which was the twos on a 3 level prison , (you really should go visit as they do tours - before it gets made into housing flats).

I had my own cell until they placed a prisoner in who attempted to murder me.

Tarlochan singh Bagri was a name I would never forget and he was my new cell mate on one of my early remands, he was also on remand

He was accused of murdering his wife in the Birmingham/wolves area 1985 , he gave me his court paperwork and asked my opinion on what I thought (being an institutionalised serial crook I would know I suppose ?).

It took me a while to read these and instantly thought "this man murdered his wife, bang to rights, he did it), Oh I forgot to mention just before I say this is that the innocent woman was strangled.

I told him about the evidence of the molten metal they retrieved from his furnace he worked at and residues of melted gold and platinum found on his uniform, the money transferred the previous day plus some I have forgot which made the man "in my eyes" a murderer.

He being banged up with me didn't worry me in the slightest as we were all innocent until proven guilty.

When I told him about what I thought about his crime he flicked me with a rat's tale (wet towel rolled up).

I flicked back on the one I quickly made, and so the play rats tale fight began, he got me, I got him and fucking hell it hurt, not as much as when he got me around the neck with his towel and started to choke me, I mean this was choking, I tried to grab his arms, tried to kick his legs from under him and push him back onto the door but he was a big lad and kept throttling.

I managed to grab the metal framed chair and with both hands swung it up over my head , luckily it landed well , the wooden seat clanked right on his forehead and for that brief second I broke free , turned around whilst his hands where on his face and gave him the biggest kick to his bollocks , the look on his face was hysterical , eyes bulging out of his fat head whilst his hands went down to the floor I grabbed the chair again and hit him around the back , I then started to bang on the 9" metal door until a screw came and opened up , I explained he tried to murder me , the screw was laughing so I barged past him until he grabbed me and took me serious .

He told me later in interview with the governor he was laughing because of the large size 22 Indian doubled over and blood pouring from his head was on the floor whilst 5 foot nothing me was scratch free ?

Err he slipped on that their bar of soap Gv'ner, honest

That man was sentenced to 15 years in prison 1 year later for the murder of his wife.

Looking at the photos of the arranged marriage when we were padded up together I really do not know how he could have done that, she was a really beautiful young looking lady who did not deserve to die, I still after 35 years think of her often and still shed a tear for her when I'm alone

Sorry going off track again , I have to tell you about my first prison sentence crime as I would feel the book would be incomplete (no doubt its massively incomplete anyway)but I can't seem to find the paperwork for it , I have no police records in what vehicle I stole or the reports do not state what it was , I would have a memory jog and tell you all about it , this is annoying as I am thinking to hard again , time for a rest as I see that when I arrived in court they had a few more charges for me to attend with , namely a house burglary ? , and more car thefts? , I am sure I will find out very soon.

After 2 weeks of reading reports whilst being in this pointless lockdown I am now starting to really regret every crime I have done in the past to the point that I think am suffering from it mentally, they will just not go from my thoughts, when I'm jogging, driving to some secluded area to write or waking up at 2am and being an insomniac for the rest of the night? , I have mentioned the crying many times in my past life but I seem to be doing it more now than I have done since my beloved Amanda passed away.

I cannot put it down to my recent break up (3 year relationship) , even though Joanne takes up my thinking every 15 minutes of my waking day and (quite often) I have to shout at myself for thinking about her more than I do of my Amanda ,(is it really possible to fall in love with 2 women ?), maybe I'm being a fool or it could be the seclusion or of me not meeting family but I think I have to put it down to the people who lost out because of my stupidity when I was this old in life , some of these crimes I have read about now which I committed around the 17/18 years old time are anus and I didn't think I was capable of doing this sort of thing , I really did not know what happened to me mentally in those days but it was not good , I think the same as my mental state now , not good , so excuse me if my writing style changes (good excuse to get a ghost writer to finish this now and me bugger off to unlock down Cyprus again , not a chance of that happening though is there).

Let's get back to my life and say that my true crime spree started around here but OUT of the arms of the carers.

I appeared at court a total of 4 times in 1 month whilst being on remand and they kept adjourning but eventually I got 42 weeks youth custody, if you could read what I'm reading about the two and fromming from courts it would crack you up, always with the same lad plus we are joined by another lad on sentencing who helped out driving the getaway car from another smash and grab in a souped up car at Majors clothes store in Shrewsbury.

On that occasion we got caught trying to break into another car in the greyfiers car park as the car we ram raided with was a front end write off by the time we got 100yrds from the shop , we legged it to the next nearest biggest car park , we did manage to get into a ford escort mk2 but collared as we were hot wiring it and turning the engine , what a bummer as this would then be take and drive away , I tell the wankknob to just stash the clothes and we would come back but oh no we wanted that jacket worth £200.00 , Caught & court .

So it was off to my first Youth custody, I had done a remand prison term for a month and a half and mingling with adult con's so I should be ok going to a teenager's prison – surely.

Unlike detention centre (Eastwood park) I did not cry , I knew the score , I was stronger than that and just nearly being murdered I was sure I could cope with what this place was about to throw at me , BUT I have never mingled with teenage "coming on" adult scousers or mancunian's before .

```
Mr T. W. Draycott,
c/o H. M. Youth Custody Centre,
Stoke Heath,
Nr. Market Drayton,
Shropshire.                                    19th November, 1984.


C.2412/3/JAW/JC                                222393   Miss J. Waring

Dear Timothy,

        Now that you are at Stoke Heath, I need to come and see you to
discuss plans for your future.

        I will be coming to see you on Friday 23rd November, and will be
bringing Mrs Wedge who is to be your probation officer.

        We will be able to discuss plans for your future with Mrs Wedge,
particularly where you are going to live when you are released.

        Looking forward to seeing you on Friday.

                        Best Wishes,
```

Well, that's it, that is the final written report by my social worker who has been my lifeline to outside life for the past 6 years, I remember her so well, always kind and would do the best for me, yes I suppose I was a right twat towards her and if you are out there Mrs Waring and reading this thinking "I knew that little twat ", well I'm sorry and i rally mean that xx.

Also massive apologies to the 70s / 80s folk of Shrewsbury , surrounding area's and especially Castlefields residents whose driveways and car parks where so tempting (as they mainly run downhill towards the main road, so easy to roll cars away)

Big Apologies to the Abusers out there , who no doubt through this memoir may be found out by investigatory reporters who I got told like to investigate books like mine for a kick and may look for the hidden subliminal clues I have left throughout the book with the abusers names .

Until the next Time..maybe XX

Printed in Great Britain
by Amazon